Alison Simone is a qualified counsellor and lives in Cheshire.

Having experienced some of the issues raised in this book and herself benefiting from counselling, Alison then felt empowered to improve her own situation and so embraced adult learning in her later years.

Becoming qualified as a counsellor, allowed for a sense of reason and purpose, and so now, Alison wishes to share this positive energy with others by furnishing them with the tools and knowledge that they too can achieve, similarly, and so bring about inner peace.

This book is dedicated to anyone who has ever found themselves in a ditch, with no tools to dig themselves out.

Its contents offer the reader a practical approach to taking repossession of their own brain, by merging various psychological theories in an easy-to-understand logic, thus giving the reader the tools needed to emerge from that ditch.

Alison Simone

IT IS MY GARDEN! SO, I SHALL TEND TO IT MYSELF

A Self-Help Book

AUSTIN MACAULEY PUBLISHERS™
LONDON • CAMBRIDGE • NEW YORK • SHARJAH

Copyright © Alison Simone 2023

The right of Alison Simone to be identified as author of this work has been asserted by the author in accordance with sections 77 and 78 of the Copyright, Designs and Patents Act 1988.

All rights reserved. No part of this publication may be reproduced, stored in a retrieval system, or transmitted in any form or by any means, electronic, mechanical, photocopying, recording, or otherwise, without the prior permission of the publishers.

Any person who commits any unauthorised act in relation to this publication may be liable to criminal prosecution and civil claims for damages.

A CIP catalogue record for this title is available from the British Library.

ISBN 9781398469556 (Paperback)
ISBN 9781398469563 (ePub e-book)

www.austinmacauley.com

First Published 2023
Austin Macauley Publishers Ltd®
1 Canada Square
Canary Wharf
London
E14 5AA

Preface

Imagine if you will a barren field, void of any foliage or vegetation, and without a surrounding fence or barrier of any sort.

Then compare this vision to that of a newborn baby's brain, vacant of stimulus, and awaiting contribution from external forces (being that of the caregiver).

As one of the first abilities a newborn gain is their sight, the first visual contribution received could be one of either a smile or a scowl, therefore the message the newborn will receive and absorb will be one of either positivity or negativity.

Let us now then connect any positive messages received to the image of a beautiful rose, and similarly, negative messages to the image of an invading weed, with either of these being planted in our barren brain field at any given time.

The more positive reinforcement a person receives as he/she grows would result in producing a beautiful blooming rose garden in our brain, although in comparison, of course, negative messages and negative reinforcement would similarly produce a dismal view, of neglected wasteland, with many weeds.

Over time, all of these contributions would equally establish themselves, creating roots, and taking ownership of their designated space. Therefore, the holder of this brain lives their life according to how many roses and how many weeds have been planted.

Introduction

This book is split into four sections in order to cover all aspects of our being, namely: physical, mental, emotional, and spiritual.

People can find that they are struggling for various reasons, this can include trauma (which was experienced as a child or as an adult), grieving (the loss of a person close to them, or loss of a way of life), or even debility, due to loss of control over their own life.

All or some aspects of our being can be affected as a result of an uncomfortable experience, be that physical, mental, emotional, or spiritual, hence the reason we will be exploring all of the above, to bring them into alignment and so create harmony within.

Our physical self is our 'being', our mental self is our 'thinking', our emotional self is our 'feelings', and our spiritual self is our 'knowing'.

Have you ever heard the saying, 'They're not firing on all four cylinders?' (A cylinder is the power unit of a car engine and it is the chamber where the petrol/gasoline is burned and turned into power). Cars have a minimum of four cylinders, (although they can have six or eight to produce more power).

So, this is simply referring to someone not functioning at the greatest possible level.

Therefore, we can liken our existence to having four cylinders, and to be functioning at our greatest possible level, all our four cylinders (Physical, Mental, Emotional and Spiritual) need to be given the same amount of thought and attention.

Physically, we will explore the changes that take place in the brain through creating an awareness of neuroplasticity, breaking old destructive thought habits, and introducing new positive thought patterns. This results in creating new neural pathways and also allows the old pathways to disconnect, through no longer being in use. (If you do not use it – you lose it!). We will also explore how struggling with anxiety or depression can possibly develop into a self-loathing of our physical self, including eating disorders or possibly body dysmorphia, and so have an adverse effect on our body.

Mentally, you can recite mantras to initiate the growth of these new neural pathways, allowing you to break the habit of returning to the previous way of thinking. A mantra is simply the practice of repeating the same words over and over (repetition is the mother of all learning!).

Emotionally, we connect to our feelings, paying attention to our instincts and doing what 'feels' right, rather than what we 'think' is right for ourselves. All too often, people do what they think is best for other people, instead of 'feeling' what is best for themselves. This then results in a feeling of neglect of oneself.

And lastly, spiritually, as we become aware of our inner strength, which we can learn to rely on to promote 'self-care', putting our own needs first and foremost. This can be achieved by mindfulness, or simply connecting to the gap in between a stimulus and our response.

Between stimulus and response, there is a space. In that space is our power to choose our response, in our response lies our growth and our freedom (Frankl, 2004).

We then use this space to decide on an outcome that is in our best interest. We must look after ourselves in the same way we look after others, although we must make this a priority to ensure our own wellbeing.

Promoting self-care is not selfish, it is a necessity, and when you begin to look after yourself you can gain hope and trust, in a brighter future, and in yourself, to do what is right for you and so achieve positive change.

Section One
Physical

In this first section, I choose to focus on the physical aspect of our being, associating these already established roots, with that of the neural pathways in the brain, this is to give the reader an understanding of how this example relates to our physical self, and how this affects our mental and emotional state of being. The brain can be described as a physical blob of muscle sitting inside our skull and dictating our thoughts and decisions. Something you think you have no control over, are the victim of and are at the mercy of its choices and judgements.

And, up until this point, you could be forgiven for thinking that!

The good news is, due to a breakthrough in research, scientists now believe we can, in fact, have control over the physical structure of our own brain, and because of this breakthrough, in 2008, Dr Norman Doidge M. D. wrote a book entitled, *The Brain That Changes Itself*, in which he focuses on the concept of Neuroplasticity.

From this book, we discover that it has been since the seventeenth century that doctors and scientists believed that the brain was rigid and that the common belief was, after childhood, the brain physically changed only when we reached our senior years, and so then it began the long process of deterioration and shrinkage. It was also accepted by these professionals that when brain cells did not initially develop properly, became injured or died off, they were never able to be replaced.

This belief of 'the static brain' commanded that people who were born with limited brain function, or who sustained brain damage, would be forever restricted from leading a full life for the remainder of their life.

But, thankfully because of this further research, it is now understood that the brain can, in fact, develop and change, due to its own plasticity, which is now known as, *Neuroplasticity*. We can now embrace the knowledge that our brain has the ability to change throughout our entire life. Neural pathways associated with a given function, which have been damaged or have developed because of particular messages received can be reassigned to a different location, and new neural pathways will eventually grow and strengthen, taking on this newly assigned responsibility.

Now for the science bit. The human brain is made up of an estimated 100 billion neurons making a total of 100 trillion neural connections. The pathways along which information travels through the neurons (nerve cells) of the brain can be compared to that of a man-made path across a field of tall grass. As people keep taking the same route across this field, they wear out a path and so every time we learn something new, these neural circuits are altered in our brain.

This then takes us back to our roses and weed roots scenario, so any of these given messages you have received will have caused structural changes in your brain to become part of how you live your life. Although, as previously stated, because of neuroplasticity, you can now *choose* to change your brain, and so *choose* to rid yourself of these weeds in your brain garden.

So, to begin with, imagine you have been given the responsibility of cultivating this piece of wasteland; your initial reaction could be one of feeling overwhelmed when you take in a possible view of total devastation. Therefore, initially, you need to identify the source of these weeds and set about not allowing any more to invade your garden.

The first thing you need to identify is the necessity to set up personal boundaries, and to do this you can visualise erecting a fence around our brain garden, making it tall, solid, and strong. This fence can represent your personal boundary and prevent you from taking ownership of any further unwanted negative messages (weeds), which are being projected toward you from others.

I am hoping that as you are reading this book; you have been able to set aside some time for yourself and so are able to participate in any suggestion made to enable these changes to begin.

Now, if you can, I need you to take some minutes out to close your eyes and really focus on the picture of your brain garden. Visualise the roses and weeds I mentioned earlier, with the amount of each according to how many negative or positive messages you have received, up until this point in your life. You need now to visualise erecting this fence, so imagine you have a piece of wood, next proceed to drive it into the earth around the edges of your brain garden, with force gained from the inner strength that you will find located deep within yourself. Continue around in the same way and then with each additional piece of wood you erect, your inner strength will become more and more familiar until your fence is finally complete. Next, visualise yourself taking a step back so you can take in all of this scene with your peripheral vision, savouring the significance of the personal boundary you have just created, and accomplished yourself.

After you have participated in this mindfulness exercise, take a moment to appreciate what you just achieved, namely the first step in instigating control!

To further explain the need to set up these personal boundaries, I will now clarify how not having them up until this point has allowed for the weeds to take up this space.

Initially, babies rely on caregivers for their survival, although as they grow and become more independent, they begin to look to themselves for their own guidance. If this is encouraged, they can begin to trust their judgement, although if they are given messages that dismiss their decisions as wrong, this is where self-doubt originates, and they possibly continue to live their lives from this point from an 'external locus of evaluation'.

So, outside of the fence you have recently erected represents the external locus (other people) and within the confines of your personal boundary fence is the 'internal locus of evaluation' (your own thoughts and decisions).

The term, '*Locus of Evaluation*', was introduced by Carl Rogers who was an American psychologist in the 1950s and is one of a series of ideas that formed a Person-Centred Approach to therapy.

This theory helps us understand that where we look for our conditions of worth can affect our self-confidence, self-esteem, and general mental health.

Carl Rogers said that if a person is operating from an internal locus of evaluation, then they trust their own instincts, that is, they use their intuitive valuing process. However, initially, many people learn to operate from an external locus of evaluation, meaning they absorb the values of others, which is the unconscious adoption of the ideas or attitudes of their caregivers. Therefore, these conditions of worth are acquired in our childhood.

Unfortunately, children can also learn by observing, and so any visual messages people received when they were young are still planted as seeds (weeds) of self-doubt, these weeds then lay dormant until triggered in later life.

Harmful words heard in adult life from a negative partner or parent can trigger these childhood memories, and cause the already established weeds to multiply, resulting in feelings of low self-esteem and low self-worth.

Ideally, a way to resolve this situation would be to promote self-care and alienate yourself physically from the source of these triggers, to prevent further affirmations of negative thoughts, and of course to repair the damage already done.

Although sometimes this is not possible, so separating yourself from this person emotionally is the next best step. Realising that you are your own gardener and that you *can choose* not to absorb their negativity.

This can be achieved by participating in mindful mantra exercises, to send positive messages to the brain, and so creating new positive neural pathways through positive affirmations, whilst also eliminating already established negative neural pathways (weeds) through lack of attention.

Remember, this is neuroplasticity doing its work, if it helps, visualise this as the roots of weeds dying off, due to lack of nourishment.

So how do you begin to shift this locus of evaluation from external to internal, which is going to lead to higher self-esteem and confidence? Well, mindfulness is one of the most accessible ways of creating this change in focus, meaning that in most situations, you can take a moment to stop what you are hearing from others and check-in with yourself to assess how you are feeling. This grounding awareness allows you time to think and capture what you are experiencing internally because what we hear from ourselves and what we are feeling can help us make decisions that can lead to promoting self-care. Over time, this results in increased self-worth because you are giving yourself time to listen to you! And although this is not easy to do at first and takes practice, eventually it can become second nature.

Awareness can help you change the way you perceive and react to moment-to-moment events as they unfold. This shift takes place when you go from thinking about the situation to simply observing. By observing, you can learn to create this gap between the stimulus and response, and this then gives you the time you need to *choose* a response that best suits you! A way in which to remember to do this is to recite the mantra, *Observe Don't Absorb, Observe Don't Absorb,* when in the company of someone who is inclined to project negativity. This technique of only observing a stimulus but not emotionally absorbing it was devised by Ross Rosenberg who credits the discovery of this technique for saving him, in his book, *The Human Magnet Syndrome: Why We Love People Who Hurt Us.*

Verbal criticism we hear externally, projected from others says nothing about us, but in fact, says more about them! This could include visual expressions of resentment or anger etc.

Psychological projection is a theory in psychology in which humans defend themselves against their own unconscious impulses or qualities (both positive and negative) by denying their existence in themselves while attributing them to others! For example, a person who is constantly rude may accuse other people of being rude. This incorporates blame-shifting!

Meaning, when a person has uncomfortable thoughts or feelings, they project these onto other people, assigning them to a convenient alternative target. Projecting these thoughts or emotions onto others allows the other person freedom from their own judgement of themselves, without feeling the discomfort of knowing that these thoughts and emotions are their own!

So, projection is the presentation of a person's undesirable thoughts, feelings, or impulses onto another person, who does not have those attributes and is used especially when these thoughts make them feel completely uncomfortable.

The next time you feel at the mercy of someone else's insults or criticism, visualise them holding onto a huge fireball and then throwing it toward you (them holding onto their fireball of hurt, anger and pain and is obviously causing them discomfort!) they want rid of it, and to rid themselves of these uncomfortable feelings they are letting you have it! Literally! But these are their own issues, which they must not simply project onto others, but identify and explore and so reach peace within themselves, therefore, you refuse to catch this fireball! And you further visualise this fireball stopping dead in front of you and dropping to the floor, like in the bullet scene in the movie, *The Matrix*, with Keanu Reeves. If you have not already watched this movie, I would recommend you do, if only to see Keanu's expression whilst refusing to absorb these bullets.

The aim here then, is to understand that when you are being insulted or verbally attacked by another, this is about them and not you! And not to accept the other person's issues and with mindfulness, you can achieve this! 'Mindfulness is awareness' and as you become more aware of the relationship between stimulus and response when something happens; you won't allow yourselves to react automatically!

This process usually happens so quickly and naturally that we are not even aware of it. For example, when someone cuts you off on the road, you instantly react to that event, but do you get to *choose* how you react? Our impulsive reaction is a habit that has been formed by repetition, but which can be broken! It is so natural for us to simply react that there is no awareness there is a gap in between stimulus and response, and so mindfulness is a tool then that will help you to identify this gap.

Stimulus | Response. Stimulus |*GAP*| Response.

All our freedom is found within that gap, in that space, you get to decide how you want to react to life as it presents itself. Mindfulness then will free you from this habit, by reflecting on a situation and then responding how you *choose* to, and not simply automatically.

Try and remember a conversation you had with someone, and afterwards, you regretted agreeing to do something for them. Next, imagine that had you been aware of the above mantra and had instigated it during this exchange, how different would that outcome have been?

Finding this gap is being aware of your personal boundaries and promoting self-care, which is what you must do if you are to look after yourself. Do not ever feel that by refusing to agree to all requests asked of you, you are not being a nice person! Because all you are *choosing* to do is to look after yourself, and you are allowed to do that!

Another way of dealing with projection is to perform the Cancel, Clear, Delete affirmation, which is known as the sorcerer's sweep and involves using your dominant hand.

Beginning at your heart position you sweep your hand away from you, then upwards, and finally over towards the back of your head. As you do so, you recite the words CANCEL (at your heart position) CLEAR (as you sweep your hand outward) and DELETE as your hand carries on up and over your head.

This action is to be performed three times rapidly, as you recite the affirmation.

This is by way of not allowing another's words or actions to be absorbed by you and so are not able to affect your energy level negatively.

The more time you spend promoting self-care will bring about quicker results, so like any task you take on, it will require dedication and commitment. You have made the first step by *choosing* to read this book, and everything begins with a *choice*. Whether you selected it yourself or someone else recommended it! So now, identify that becoming aware of this *choice* you made is an element of mindfulness. Reflect on that for a moment, you made a decision to do something that you hope will benefit you, you thought about you! Thinking about the reasons you do things is mindfulness.

Each time I have used the word *choose, choice* or *chosen* I have highlighted it in italics, and the reason for this is, as I specified earlier, everything begins with a choice! Without mindful awareness, you can go through your days being carried on the crest of a wave, and when evening time comes, you find yourself wondering how you got yourself into a particular situation? Suffice to say, you were not aware that you had a choice to decide on the outcome of the day's events! All too often, it appears that the 'little voice in your head' seems to be making your decisions for you, and at present, you feel you have no control over that voice. So, what if I were to tell you that it is not actually a voice? But simply a thought, and possibly a negative thought at that!

A negative automatic thought (or NATs for short) is a term used by Arron Beck and Albert Ellis in Cognitive Behavioural Therapy (CBT) who described them as a stream of thoughts that you will notice because you *choose* to pay attention to them. They are negative explanations of what you think is happening to you, and they generally have an impact on your feelings and emotions, which is not positive!

Let us now associate these negative thoughts with the weeds in our brain garden, and to the negative messages we received whilst growing up. Those messages that made you feel you were not good enough, beautiful enough, clever enough, etc, and so every time you were put into a situation where you had to prove your worth, you were unable to, because these negative thoughts jumped straight in, automatically telling you not to bother, there is no point, and that you would probably embarrass yourself anyway!

Don't you just wish you could stop listening to these thoughts?

What if I told you that you can! And it begins with a *choice*!

Up until now, these negative thoughts have possibly controlled your decision making because you have given them control! But this is where you can *choose* to take that control back.

At this point, I would like you to participate in another mindfulness exercise, and this time I would like you to visualise your brain garden, complete with the personal boundary fence you erected earlier, standing tall, sturdy, and proud. But this time also visualise the roses and weeds and take in how many of each there are? Next, if you identify a negative thought you have had recently and assign it to one of these weeds, then see yourself pulling up that weed and tossing it over your fence. You are making the *choice* not to have it invading the space in your brain garden anymore! Do this as many times as you feel you need to, because eventually, of course, we want to see all roses and no weeds!

Each time you hear something derogatory from yourself, recall this vision and recall pulling up and discarding that weed to oblivion. Associate all negative thoughts to weeds, which you do not wish to own, because the more time you give to these weeds, the more you are nourishing them and allowing them to remain alive. *Choosing* not to, is depriving them of sustenance and like everything else, if you ignore it, it goes away! And of course, you can look to neuroplasticity for this confirmation.

As Norman Doidge says, *'These weeds will die off when you cease spending time on them',* he also confirms that a person's own thoughts can physically change the brain, decreasing negative neural pathways, whilst creating new neural pathways with positive thinking; so similarly, you can choose to plant more roses!

For you to begin this process, I would ask now for you to take time out from reading this book, and write two lists, the first of which will be entitled, 'Ten things I am proud of about myself' and the second being, 'Ten things I like about myself'.

'What?' I hear you say. 'I can't think of ten!' No, not off the top of your head you will not be able to! But what I am asking is for you to delve deep into your memory bank and reconnect with times throughout your life, in your childhood even, when you accomplished something that made you feel good. The second list can include physical attributes and personality traits, and once you have written these lists, I advise that you read through them slowly, giving each contribution a few moments of your time for you to be able to reflect on that memory, and reconnect with your feelings and emotions on that occasion.

How did that feel? Did you feel proud whilst remembering?

Did you feel proud whilst identifying your good attributes?

That emotion of pride is what grows the roses in your brain garden, so keep these lists handy and read them daily as affirmations! First thing in the morning and possibly last thing at night too! And know that as you are doing this, you are physically creating new neural pathways in your brain. Visualise this happening and know that your roses are your new neural pathways, connect to this vision as you are reading through your lists because you are now in control of what takes up the space in your brain garden! And you can choose what grows there, what flourishes, and what dies off!

In addition to people you meet projecting their issues and causing discomfort, it is advisable to identify when your emotions are being triggered unintentionally by others. Something someone says that has no malicious intent could suddenly cause uneasiness within you, and so through mindful awareness, you could then identify this as a trigger.

Although what exactly do we mean by a trigger?

The dictionary definition is: '*A trigger is an event that is the cause of a particular action, process or situation.*'

You may even be unaware that you have a problem, until something or someone 'triggers' a memory that causes panic or anxiety, or even sudden darkness in the mood. Some memories can be related to historic trauma from childhood, but once this memory is uncovered and you now have an awareness of it, you are now able to *choose* to not allow these same words to initiate distress within you, and then decide to resolve this issue by a variety of means.

Self-exploration is another concept of mindfulness, this is when you decide to take time out and explore how it was that an external stimulus created such a profound effect on your emotions. Through this exploration, you could possibly uncover some uncomfortable truths, which then results in you identifying an issue that up until the point of receiving the trigger, you subconsciously chose to bury and ignore.

Unfortunately, if you simply decide to be like an ostrich and bury your head in the sand, people and situations still have the opportunity to kick your protruding butt! And so, although you think you have dealt with a problem, you are still vulnerable to discomfort. Hence, the trigger reaches unresolved wounds.

Deciding to face any identified issues is the first step on the road to wholeness, which of course takes courage, and the definition of courage is?

Feeling afraid but doing it anyway! In spite of your fear.

In addition to feeling out of sorts as a reaction to triggers, you can also identify that with each experience you have witnessed or have been involved in creates a chemical reaction in your brain, and depending on what experience that is, whether it be pleasurable or painful it can either increase or decrease a particular chemical level and too much is as bad as too little! I am sure you have heard the saying, 'You can get too much of a good thing!' Also, 'All things in moderation!' Well, that applies to our brain chemicals, which is why when people become over-excited, they feel lightheaded or dizzy, and this is because of a sudden surge or drop in a particular chemical due to whatever activity you are participating in.

So, bearing that in mind, this brings us to another element of self-help and planting more roses.

Each time you praise yourself or acknowledge self-achievement, you are increasing your 'feel good' chemicals namely, *Serotonin and Dopamine*, and so raising their levels! You may not have initially had control over the level reduction due to negative experiences, but you do have control over the increase in level!

A theory put forward by Pepperell (2018), says, '*We could account for all the complex processes occurring in the brain in terms of energy, forces at work that is: physical, chemical, and biological processes.*'

Now in order to explain the difference between these feel-good chemicals – Serotonin and Dopamine, imagine sinking into a nice hot bath after a long tiring day at work, especially if you have created ambience and added essential oil to the bathwater, and possibly lit an incense stick and some candles! This does not only signify romance, but it also signifies pampering! (Or of course, standing underneath a refreshing shower!) Also, then slipping between clean fresh sheets afterwards, this 'Aww' feeling of happiness, relaxation and contentment is the surge of Serotonin in your brain.

Although Dopamine is more linked to an exciting feeling, the way you would feel if you were just about to come first in a race, going on a theme park ride or if you are expecting nice presents at Christmas, also looking forward to going on a holiday that you have possibly planned all year. Although too much excitement can result in a huge surge of Dopamine, which is why people (children mainly) can become nauseous when excited. So, to clarify, Serotonin is connected to happiness and contentment, and Dopamine is connected to excitement and enthusiasm.

You have probably heard the saying, 'You are what you eat', well you can increase your Serotonin and Dopamine levels by eating certain foods, below is a list of foods to include in your daily diet when wishing to partake in this exercise.

To Increase Serotonin:	To Increase Dopamine:
Spinach,	Ripe Bananas,
Turnip,	Apples,
Bananas,	Strawberries,
Pineapples,	Prunes,
Kiwi Fruit,	Blueberries,

Plums, Almonds,
Eggs, Natural Probiotic, Yoghurt.

For even more information on how to increase these chemicals, check out [GoodTherapy.org.].

Now here comes another science bit! This is also exactly what SSRIs do! (Selective Serotonin Reuptake Inhibitors or Anti-Depressants). Raymond Goldberg explains to us that these tablets help to increase the levels of serotonin in the brain (in the synaptic gap) by inhibiting re-absorption during synapses. Similarly, Norepinephrine-Dopamine Reuptake Inhibitors (NDRIs) work with the neurotransmitters, *Norepinephrine and Dopamine*, although they have a different effect than SSRIs. (Oh, neurotransmitters are chemicals that act as messengers in the brain!).

NDRIs would not be the first choice of tablets prescribed for depression by doctors though and would only be prescribed when other tablets such as SSRIs have been unsuccessful in relieving symptoms of depression.

This solution of taking prescribed medication for depression only treats the symptoms, and not the cause though, (the cause being the experience which lowered the levels initially) which is why anti-depressants can only be considered as a short-term fix as opposed to long term, which would be to resolve the cause through exploration. Although there are instances where people have become dependent on these tablets and so see this as long term, but there is still a way back! Doctors can instigate the weaning off process if they deem this appropriate, should anyone wish to try the alternative route of self-help or counselling.

In order to link up what has been covered up until this point, we can identify projection and the absorption of projection, as living from an external locus of evaluation (by owning these opinions and insults) although, once you have made the *choice* to find the gap and not automatically react or absorb, you will then be choosing to live from an internal locus of evaluation.

This can also be applied to where you identify your happiness comes from! If you connect the responsibility of our happiness only to external situations i.e., looking forward to various events, which could include a wedding or birthday celebration or the birth of a child etc, to name a few, or being with a partner, then it would follow that if you did not have any of the above happening now or in the near future, you would have nothing to look forward to or focus on. So, in order to shift this direction to an internal responsibility, you could look at ways of creating your own happiness and becoming personally responsible for your own sense of fulfilment.

But how? I hear you say! Well, in order to begin this process, again, of course, it begins with a *choice*! You choose that you want to be happy, and from that foundation, you set about putting your plan into action, and as this is the physical section of this book, I will focus on what physical aspects you can give attention to, to be able to increase a feeling of wellbeing, before moving onto other mental health struggles that affect your physicality.

So, taking into consideration Endorphins are another feel-good chemical, and these are released in our brains when we exercise, resulting in a positive feeling in our body. Then it follows that if you decide to join a gym, go jogging alone or with a friend, or simply purchase some exercise equipment to use at home, these activities are going to initiate this. You do not even have to associate this decision with losing weight or getting fit! It is simply about producing feel-good chemicals in your brain, but of course, if you keep at it, you will possibly lose weight and get fitter! So that is another bonus to be happy about, which will produce more Serotonin, so it is a win-win situation. And you have probably heard this other saying of, 'If it feels good, do it!' So, do it! And afterwards, you can participate in either taking a hot relaxing bath or shower, which will, of course, result in even more serotonin production.

Although the advice here, of course, is everything in moderation because you can get too much of a good thing! So, although you need to remember not to exert yourself, it is good to know what Dr William Bloom tells us that endorphins themselves are not addictive or damaging.

We see ourselves every day, whether that be deliberately, whilst doing our hair or make-up and checking our clothes are sitting correctly, in a mirror at home, or by accident whilst out, when passing shop windows or mirrors in an acquaintance's home. Whether you like what you see physically or not depends on how you are feeling at that precise moment, judging by what is affecting you mentally, emotionally, and spiritually.

Sometimes people can project their own hurt, anger, or pain inwardly, onto themselves bodily, as opposed to projecting it onto others. This can take many forms and can include starving themselves (Anorexia) because they think they are too fat, although that reason can sometimes be masking a feeling of a lack of control over their lives and so by controlling the consumption of food is one area where they feel they are having at least some control. Or even Bulimia

Nervosa, which involves binge eating, and refers to someone eating a vast amount of food in a short space of time. Although binging is then followed by purging, which refers to the person's attempts to get rid themselves of the food they have recently consumed, by vomiting or taking laxative tablets.

Some people, when feeling in a low level of mood possibly due to stress, will often turn to food for comfort, this is referred to as comfort eating or emotional eating. Although if they struggle with Bulimia Nervosa, once the food has been digested, they instinctively feel guilty or afraid in respect of putting on weight. This could either be as a result of pressure from society in general, to be thin or possibly having been judged or criticised at some point in their life regarding their weight. Either way, they then feel they have to reverse the process, hence the purging. This becomes a vicious cycle and could even result in Anorexia Nervosa, as someone can, in fact, struggle with both of these eating disorders at the same time.

Anorexia can be linked to body dysmorphia, and this is another area in which experiencing trauma can manifest itself on the physical self. Body Dysmorphic Disorder, commonly known as BDD causes sufferers to ruminate over their seemingly physical defect for several hours a day, and so possibly restricts their eating habits, in addition, they avoid all social activities, camouflage their perceived defect with cosmetics or clothing, repetitively checks their appearance and compares themselves to others, they also avoid mirrors if they can and continually change outfits and groom excessively.

Unfortunately, people with these conditions, including obesity, are often identified as causing their own condition, so being labelled as self-inflicted, and although each of the above is all variations of self-harm, most people would only identify or attach self-injury and causing an element of pain to themselves, to this label. Although it is good to note that explanations for these conditions go far deeper than simple greed or vanity.

Self-harm does not only include 'cutting', but there are also many other ways to intentionally cause harm, which include:

Burning of skin.

Punching or hitting.

Hair-pulling (from root).

Poisoning with tablets or toxic chemicals.

Misusing alcohol or drugs.

Lack of self-love, progressing toward self-hatred sometimes manifests into anger, and as that anger is turned inwards, so the need to punish themselves arises, this then results in a variety of methods to bring about this physical suffering.

If you, reading this book, or someone you know is struggling with either of these afflictions let it be known that there is a way back from this situation and that through exploration and self-empowerment, personal control can be instigated, with a feeling of greater self-worth being achieved.

To feel content is acknowledging that you are in control of you! Your thoughts, your decisions, your feelings, and your emotions. In retrospect, anxiety rears its ugly head when we feel out of control. Imagine anxiety had a voice; the words that voice is saying are, 'What about me?' 'What about me?'

Intuitively you know you are neglecting yourself, and so we can connect anxiety to ignoring your own wants and needs. We can also connect anxiety to the behaviour of a child, not that I am insinuating anyone with anxiety is childish! But in the respect of: if a child is in the company of his/her mother and mother is chatting on the phone and so is ignoring the child's plea for attention. The child has maybe seen something exciting or fascinating and wants to show their mother before the moment passes, so we have impatience and excitement involved in the situation. So, the child then throws a tantrum showing their unhappiness, and also in an attempt to obtain attention. Well, anxiety, in the same way, is attempting to get your attention! Trying to let you know that you are neglecting yourself, not listening to yourself and therefore not promoting self-care.

Anxiety is the ignored child, pleading to be shown attention, jumping up and down, kicking and squealing, hence the stomach cramps or butterfly sensation anxiety causes in the stomach! Or the pins and needles sensation in various parts of your body, your body is throwing a tantrum, in an attempt to be listened to!

The first step then, is to start listening to your discomfort and to your intuition. As you would ask the children throwing a tantrum, 'What is wrong?' Ask yourself the same question: Ask yourself why am I unhappy? Why do I not feel content? And identify these areas in your life where you feel uncomfortable. What you will possibly identify is that you are not in control! But it is your life, no one else's, and as an adult maturity means to take ownership, make your own decisions, and learn from your mistakes. Your life is about pleasing yourself first and foremost, taking care of yourself first and foremost, and if this is not what you are doing, and you are ignoring yourself. Make a decision to be in control, I cannot say take back or regain control, because you possibly have never been in control in the first place!

Unfortunately, due to these weeds that have been planted in your brain garden as a result of the negative messages received, this has caused an overgrowth of lack of control, so once you start the weeding-out process, you begin to take control of your own life. Up until this point, you have been an observer of your own life, rather than the controller and so from here, you begin to identify whose choices and whose decisions have led you to where you are today? And when you acknowledge they are not yours, this is where you begin to instigate the changes.

Remember the gap? Fill that gap with mantras, even if you do not believe what you say to yourself at present, you will be creating a new positive neural pathway, and the more you say something, the more you will believe it! In the same way that you believe your negative thoughts, you will begin to believe your positive thoughts! And as it is this easy, why would we choose to fill our brain garden with self-planted weeds when we can just as easily fill it with self-planted roses! So, begin today, go plant some roses, in fact, lots of roses!

It is your life and your *choice*: Bitter or Better? You can decide to continue to be bitter or to become better at listening to yourself and looking after yourself!

Learned behaviour is what has ruled up until this point, well break the chain, reroute the path, pull up the weeds and decide to be in control of your own life.

You will be teaching yourself how to like yourself, how to like what you see, and even how to love yourself, promoting self-love is freeing yourself from self-hatred.

Darkness cannot drive out darkness; only light can do that. Hate *cannot* drive out hate; *only* love *can do that.*

– Martin Luther King, Jr.

Whatever experiences you have had to endure, you can decide now to draw a line in the sand and move toward that light, do not wait for it to appear at the end of the tunnel, light up the tunnel yourself! You do not even need to point the finger or lay blame at anyone's door in order to move on, in fact, you could even choose to forgive any perpetrator, bearing in mind that this would be purely for your own benefit, and your recovery, not for any advantage to them.

Holding on to anger and hatred only serves to affect you, the person who you have these feelings for is unaffected and is possibly going about their day oblivious.

Have you often wondered how parents who have lost children in horrific circumstances can choose to forgive the person responsible? Well, that is just it, they choose to! They choose to let go of all that negative emotion and in doing so, are able to focus their attention on a more positive activity. Some have then chosen to put all that energy into setting up a charity to offer support for other parents who have experienced the same trauma, and so replacing the negative with positive they are able to heal and feel again.

Grief affects your body as well as your mind, the cliché of 'a broken heart' resonates with those who have experienced this, as a physical pain that is felt in the chest area, identifying all physical hurts are not self-inflicted. All too often they ask themselves, 'When will this end? When will this pain go away?' And yet, if we attach that to the holding on of anger, this can possibly delay the healing process.

What can also delay the healing process with grief is a variation of defence mechanisms, not wanting to feel the pain and therefore suppressing it using either denial or avoidance. Unfortunately, this can lead to depression and/or anxiety as your body is not being allowed an outlet to express this sadness and heal and anxiety in this instance is your body's way of telling you that it does not like being ignored.

Showing your emotions is NOT a sign of weakness, and the sooner the better society should overrule that thought process! But where did it derive from? How is everyone accepting this unhealthy decree?

Imagine a society out of control, mass hysteria, how could calm and control be established if the whole country is panicking?

Now imagine a being in the midst of war.

How would you feel? Scared? Petrified? Not knowing what you should do?

Next, you are being given the messages:

KEEP CALM AND CARRY ON.
KEEP A STIFF UPPER LIP.

So, what do you do? Of course, you follow guidance!

Although this guidance is telling you not to feel, and not to think! Just simply get on with things as per normal!

So, you are living in the midst of chaos! And yet you are being advised to act as if you are not!

This goes against all your natural instincts of identifying the situation as trauma, but you are being conditioned to ignore your emotions and simply conform to rules.

These rules are what have carried the stigma of expressing emotions, so we can identify where this thought process originated, and why (in an attempt to prevent mass hysteria) but that was then, and this is now, and therefore we have to change that message! If you feel you cannot keep calm and carry on, speak to someone! If you feel your upper lip does quiver, speak to someone! You are not a robot, you have thoughts and emotions, and it is okay to express them! Keeping these feelings suppressed is what leads to anxiety and depression, by not being true to yourself, and ignoring that inner voice, which is trying to tell you, *I'm not okay.*

Ill advisedly, veterans were persuaded on disembarkation to not discuss their experiences, and so, unfortunately, had to live with the effects of trauma, although fortunately those described as having battle fatigue (WW1), shell shock (WW2) were at least given some attention, also Post Traumatic Stress Disorder (PTSD, Vietnam War) which is where counselling originated.

The extent to which mental health was ignored on the battlefield resulted in those fleeing the chaos, being branded deserters and so were executed in return.

Gracefully, in 2000, all of these soldiers were posthumously pardoned.

So, forget the 'keep calm and carry on' and the 'stiff upper lip jargon', and do not ignore yourself! Speak up and let people know exactly how you are feeling.

A specific area where people struggle to speak up is if they have been subjected to physical sexual abuse. Often this is because the perpetrator uses threats or blackmail to silence their subject, other times it can be a reluctance to bring shame on the family, and so the subject of these unhealthy advances makes a choice to 'suffer in silence'. Unfortunately, the shame and guilt that is experienced by the innocent party do not go away, and so manifests in other ways including anxiety, depression, self-harm, and skin problems, possibly a number of ailments could have their root issue in sexual abuse.

Other physical conditions which affect the skin, possibly again due to internalised anger and pain (again manifesting as depression, stress, or anxiety) which are taken into account include: Acne, Eczema, Hives and Psoriasis, as Matt Traube confirms. When we do not feel safe or in control, our skin can unfortunately react. Anxiety can have an impact on the health of our skin, and for those suffering from any of these skin conditions, anxiety can cause aggravated eruptions and increase symptoms.

Fear Breeds Fear! And so being afraid of eruptions can actually cause eruptions.

Focus then should not be on the skin and ointments and medicinal remedies but by reflecting on the root cause of the anxiety.

A particular physical angle in mental health I wish to bring your attention to is that of, *The Vagus Nerve.*

'What?' I hear you express.

Well, exploration has discovered that mild stimulation of this vagus nerve could help alleviate symptoms of PTSD, which is a condition that can cause extreme anxiety.

Now get ready for another 'science bit!'

The vagus nerve is the longest of the 12 pairs of cranial nerves that stem from the brain. It transmits information to or from the surface of the brain to tissues and organs elsewhere in the body. The name 'vagus' comes from the Latin term for 'wandering'; this is because the vagus nerve wanders from the brain into organs in the neck, chest, and abdomen and has a number of different functions.

The vagus nerve key functions are:

Sensory: From the throat, heart, lungs, and abdomen.

Special sensory: Provides taste sensation behind the tongue.

Motor: Provides movement functions for the muscles in the neck responsible for swallowing and speech.

Parasympathetic: Responsible for the digestive tract, respiration, and heart rate functioning.

In addition, other effects include:

Communication between the brain and the gut: the vagus nerve delivers information from the gut to the brain.

Relaxation with deep breathing: The vagus nerve communicates with the diaphragm. With deep breaths, you feel more relaxed.

Decreasing inflammation: The vagus nerve sends an anti-inflammatory signal to other parts of the body.

Lowering the heart rate and blood pressure: If the vagus nerve is overactive, it can lead to the heart being unable to pump enough blood around the body. In some cases, excessive vagus nerve activity can cause loss of consciousness and organ damage.

Fear management: The vagus nerve sends information from the gut to the brain, which is linked to dealing with stress, anxiety, and fear (hence the saying 'gut feeling') Tom Seymour gives us reassurance telling us that these signals help a person to recover from stressful and scary situations.

So, as you can see, this is pretty much an important part of your anatomy in respect of your mental health wellbeing.

The path of the vagus nerve starts in the brain and runs down the trunk of the body, with protruding branches, which supply nerves to major organs. It touches upon the parasympathetic nervous system and so helps regulate the heart, lungs, and digestive system. This main nerve is a bi-directional nerve, meaning it both sends signals from the brain to the organs and the organs send messages back to the brain.

Compare this nerve with a dual carriageway running between two towns, with people wanting to visit and leave each town. In the event of a collision, the traffic slows down and so the journey becomes sluggish, as of course both carriageways are now not operating at their full potential.

So, the same dilemma can be applied to the vagus nerve after any bad experience or trauma, meaning that this congestion needs to be dealt with to allow things to run smoothly again.

Recovery of the vagus nerve can be resolved by yourself easily, by implementing some simple techniques repeatedly.

These techniques include:

Splashing cold water on your face.

Gargling.

Breathing in and out slowly (although forcing all of the air out of your lungs during exhaling, prior to inhaling again).

Humming.

And of course, those you have already heard of to improve wellbeing, which includes walking and exercise.

All of the above constitute removing the congestion from your vagus nerve, allowing things to run smoothly again, and so increasing positive physical and emotional welfare.

Kenneth Hugdahi emphasises that the vagus nerve is the most important nerve in the body for the Psychophysiologist as it regulates heart rate and blood pressure, which are paramount to our wellbeing. Psychophysiology is the study of the relationship between physiological and psychological phenomena (the way in which the mind and body interact). Wherein it is identified and accepted that there is a strong connection between the mind and body.

Although all of the aforementioned conditions are emotional problems caused by emotions, physical problems can also be caused by emotions! This is known as, *Psychophysiology,* and having this condition is referred to as having a Psychophysiological illness, and can include any stress-related physical illnesses, such as ulcers, headaches, high blood pressure, heart disease and also backache to name a few.

These physical ailments are believed to develop as a result of suppressing unresolved issues when people are using the defence mechanism of avoidance.

After suffering a trauma, people could identify that they 'moved on' or 'got over it', although it has been identified that unless these memories and emotions are allowed to be expressed verbally and emotionally, they will manifest physically.

To clarify how someone would express these memories verbally and emotionally, I will explain the difference. Let us identify that we are relaying the events of a situation to another person in story form, we, therefore, are detached from the emotion, possibly having become desensitised from the hurt and pain these memories evoke. Although, in order to fully heal from this pain, they need to be exercised. Oh, please do not associate this word with demons, it simply means to rid yourself of any unpleasantries.

Therefore, in order to begin this task first, you would need to introduce mindfulness in the first instance and reconnect visually to the specific moment of trauma. This is probably best done with a counsellor providing a safe and tranquil space. Although, having confirmed you have a supportive friend or relative around, who is prepared to sit and listen to you and stay with you until recovery from any emotional distress this therapeutic exercise will stir up, this could begin your healing journey. I say begin and not resolve because healing is a process, which cannot be rushed, and it will take as long as it takes. Only the person, who has experienced the trauma, will know when these memories no longer cause those issues. It may take many hours and many therapeutic interventions before healing is complete, and things do get worse before they get better! People often expect an incline in recovery and become dismayed if they 'have a bad day'. Although let us identify 'peaks' and 'troughs' in recovery from the trauma, some days will be better than others, but eventually, there will be more peaks than troughs! So do not connect with lack of improvement and instead celebrate the good days.

Visualise an empty glass, and with each trauma or severity of the trauma, a volume of water is poured into this glass. Clients come to counselling after becoming overwhelmed with life, although they are unable to pinpoint the exact cause, yet a current situation does not always present as the cause, and instead, it is an increase in the volume of an already almost full glass.

Therapy reduces this amount gradually until eventually, the glass becomes empty, and mindfulness exercises are then introduced to empty this glass regularly, each time it takes in water. But attention does need to be paid to the fact that during therapy life can get in the way of recovery, in addition to the revisiting of traumatic memories, and so sometimes it will indeed feel like a bad day.

Your emotional state may get worse before it gets better during healing but enduring this will bring about peace of mind and an ability to deal with any future issues.

Suffice to say, endurance brings about results.

Physically, your appearance may sometimes change throughout this period of emotional adjustment; this is because you are no longer suppressing these emotions and so they are visible. You may gain weight, lose weight, or look gaunt, however, when you are fully recovered you will bloom and look and of course, feel better than you have done in a very long time.

Everything begins with hope, and that hope of recovery will spur you on. Determination and dedication toward self-care will then launch you further toward your goal, and a promise to yourself of promoting personal boundaries will assist in attaining your desired outcome.

You can do this! Because you owe it to yourself, to look after yourself and protect yourself from harm, physical or mental.

You are already amazing! This is just hidden beneath pain and sorrow, but once you weed out the negative and allow yourself to blossom with the positive, nothing can stop you from achieving whatever you want for yourself. You deserve it! So go for it!

At this point, I will visit neuroplasticity again and the concept of rewiring the brain through repetition.

So, as discussed previously, the neural pathways that were created in our brain from birth do not have to stay put! And another analogy for this (likened to this age of technology in which we are present) is that of a laptop that has been passed on to you (without strings attached!). Which is not yet password protected by you.

This laptop has numerous downloads and files which have been inputted, by the previous person/s who had access to it, who, (although has transferred ownership) still persists in using it, in addition to downloading and creating new files.

This would feel very frustrating, as the laptop now belongs to you, and only you should be able to choose what information is able to be stored on the hard drive. So, the change in this situation begins with a *choice*, 'I can choose to change this'.

Secondly, could be the decision, 'I am going to change this'. So, you search through the files to filter out those which you still want to keep, and those which you wish to delete. (Other's files – External Locus of Evaluation, your choice of files to keep – Internal Locus of Evaluation).

One way in which to identify what files (beliefs) to keep, and which ones to delete is to look at the Personal construct theory, which is a theory of personality and cognition developed by an American psychologist, George Kelly in the

1950s. Once we begin to reflect on ourselves and what we consider our life choices, we can put each of these into a specific category, which includes:

Parental Constructs.

Educational Constructs.

Professional Constructs.

Relationship Constructs.

Social Constructs.

The above can be associated with living from an external locus of evaluation, so if you were to identify the reason you think a particular way, or do something in a particular way, is because this is how you were taught to/told to/advised to, by either a parent, teacher, employer, partner, or friend/ news/ magazine/ book, then once you have given these habits some consideration, you then have the *choice* to keep or delete.

The files (beliefs/habits/neural pathways) you choose to keep then fall into the category of 'Personal Constructs', and so now you are living from an Internal Locus of Evaluation. This, of course, is provided that you also password protect this laptop (personal boundaries), preventing others from inputting files without your permission and prior to your consideration and decision.

Similar to John Lennon's words, all I am saying is, give personal constructs a chance!

You can then begin to create more personal neural pathways by changing your behaviours. Similar to how you do not have to think about walking, to give any thought to this act because it has a connected neural pathway, and so to walk is simply (as you have possibly heard the phrase) 'on automatic pilot'. And yet if you were to analyse walking, we could compare this to a mindful walking meditation, which is sometimes practised prior to a sitting or lying down meditation in order to calm and ground the person. There are six steps to this exercise, which you could try out for yourself.

In a comfortable standing position, carry out the following instructions slowly:

1. Raise the hind foot (heel) off the ground.
2. Next, raise the forefoot (toe area) off the ground.
3. Lift the leg upwards slightly.
4. Move the leg forward using a comfortable size stride.
5. Place the hind foot down on the ground first.
6. Place the forefoot down on the ground second.

Of course, then repeat the process with the other leg! You can choose to walk the length of a room a few times until you feel relaxed. So, walking takes at least three different objectives, and yet no thought is given to these individual objectives, which is the clarification of neural pathway activity. Another clarification would be learning a driving route to a new job, initially, you would rely on a map, a satnav or written instructions, although eventually, you would not need any of those, as due to repetition (driving the same route every day of the week, for a month or two) you are now on automatic pilot when going to work and home again, so much so that if you have ever found yourself tired driving to work or driving home and are lacking concentration, or focusing on another task even, have you noticed you still manage to get to your destination! Well, you can thank neuroplasticity for this.

Repetition, repetition, repetition! Either thinking or doing or both bring the change you want and how long that takes depends on you! Doing something once a day for seven days is going to take longer to produce results than doing the same thing seven times for seven days!

It is said that to repeat the same phrase morning, noon, and evening, for three weeks creates a new neural connection, although to make that connection longer, stronger, and thicker (to become on 'automatic pilot') if you were to repeat it even more often, the results would be even more profound. Eventually, when neuroplasticity has taken place an awareness of this new information will be present, prior to you actually saying the phase! It will then occur to you that you did not think about the phase and that the change just happened! Your thoughts/opinions present as totally different (regarding a particular person/situation) compared to how you have thought about this in the past.

It is more difficult than it was in childhood because now you have to focus and concentrate on bringing about this change, especially if you are feeling in a low mood, and repetition can be extremely boring! Although you can make this a more interesting and acceptable practice (Breuning, 2015). One way to instigate this is to think of something you used to enjoy or still do, such as singing, dancing, walking, or skipping even, and so then once you have identified this pleasurable activity you can introduce a phrase (or mantra) here and then connect this mantra to the activity i.e.:

- Sing your mantra to the tune of a favourite song.
- Create dance moves to the beat of your mantra.
- Go for a walk and make each step a mantra step.
- Use a skipping rope to skip to your mantra.

You have now created a more agreeable acceptance to reciting this mundane mantra!

So far, we have explored what effect anxiety can have on the physical, although experiencing stress and depression can also have a hugely detrimental effect on the physical body. Generally, people are quick to accept stress as a diagnosis and yet rebuff anxiety and depression! (Although stress is the forerunner of anxiety and depression). In fact, humanity, in general, allows identity connected with stress, whilst not wanting to be associated with the stigma attached to being diagnosed with any element of mental health. And recent diagnosis for physical conditions such as Chronic Fatigue, Multiple Sclerosis (MS) and Fibromyalgia allows the population to accept these as simply a physical condition, without any possibility of a physical cure, accepting painkillers and also embracing the information that these conditions could resolve over time. People at present are choosing to accept only this and furthermore reject the suggestion that CBT Therapy or other Talking Therapies may resolve their condition. They are reluctant to make the connection between physical and mental, not wanting to admit or accept they are being affected mentally by their experiences. Yet because they are in denial about their mental state and so suppressing their emotions, this is causing their core self to shout even louder for attention by manifesting physical symptoms.

This is so unfair to their inner child who experienced mistreatment or trauma, was not heard, or listened to, and is still being ignored. So much so that the trauma manifests in the physical in desperation to have a voice.

When the stigma connected to mental health is finally destroyed, these forgotten children inside can eventually be healed.

I choose to describe the above conditions as, *Physical Depression*, and maybe attaching the term physical as a forerunner to depression the population may be more willing to accept this diagnosis, and so seek treatment for depression!

This is not to say that people would be better off refusing painkillers in favour of Talking Therapy, in the same way, that people should not be quick to come off anti-depressants when participating in therapy. Like painkillers, anti-depressants, and antibiotics, talking therapy is a course and every course only reaps results and rewards when the course is completed. So, some things are more beneficial when allowed to run alongside each other, and the client will know when they are improving physically and so are then able to discuss with their GP the possibility of reducing their intake of tablets. All medication needs to be reduced gradually due to the chemical changes in the brain that the medication causes, and so implementing a gradual end rather than an abrupt end will allow the brain chemicals to adjust slowly to these implemented changes. And of course, the reduction in the physical symptoms as a result of paying attention to the mental causes will bring about the solution the client hoped for.

To elaborate further on the above conditions, the symptoms for each are:

Fibromyalgia.

Widespread pain.

Increased sensitivity to pain.

Extreme tiredness (fatigue).

Muscle stiffness.

Difficulty sleeping.

Problems with mental processes (known as, *fibro-fog*), such as problems with memory and concentration.

Headaches.

Irritable bowel syndrome (IBS), is a digestive condition that causes stomach pain and bloating.

Chronic Fatigue Syndrome (CFS):

The main symptom of CFS is feeling extremely tired and generally unwell.

Sleep problems.

Muscle or joint pain.

Headaches.

A sore throat or sore glands that are not swollen.

Problems thinking, remembering, or concentrating.

Flu-like symptoms.

Feeling dizzy or sick.

Fast or irregular heartbeats (heart palpitations).

Most people find over exercising makes their symptoms worse.

The severity of symptoms can vary from day to day, or even within a day.

Multiple sclerosis (MS):

This can cause a wide range of symptoms and affect any part of the body. Each person with the condition is affected differently. The symptoms are unpredictable. Some people's symptoms develop and worsen steadily over time, while for others they come and go. Periods, when symptoms get worse, are known as relapses. Periods, when symptoms improve or disappear, are known as remissions.

Some of the most common symptoms include:

- Fatigue.
- Vision problems.
- Numbness and tingling.
- Muscle spasms, stiffness, and weakness.
- Mobility problems.
- Problems with thinking, learning, and planning.
- Depression and anxiety.
- Sexual problems.
- Bladder problems.
- Bowel problems.
- Speech and swallowing difficulties.

Most people with MS only have a few of these symptoms.

Although feeling fatigued is one of the most common and troublesome symptoms of MS. It is often described as an overwhelming sense of exhaustion, which means it is a struggle to carry out even the simplest activities. Fatigue can significantly interfere with your daily activities and tends to get worse towards the end of each day, in hot weather, after exercising, or during illness.

Please see your GP if you are worried you might have early signs of MS. The symptoms can be similar to several other conditions, so they are not necessarily caused by MS.

One way to gain control over any of these symptoms is to introduce mindfulness, whenever you experience pain choose to stop what you are doing immediately, find a comfortable sitting or lying down position and before reaching for the painkillers, begin to visualise pleasant images, these could be memories or holidays yet to come. Each and every time you feel a pang of pain or discomfort during this period of time retaliate with a joyful opposite! What you are doing here is sending signals to the brain to interrupt the message of pain and replace it with a signal of happiness. Eventually, through persistence, you will overpower these pains and take back control over your body to enable you to continue with the task at hand.

I identify that each newborn is filled with one hundred percent of pure love energy when they enter the physical realm. Parents have often said at the point of birth that they have felt an overwhelming feeling of love when first being introduced to their newborn; this could be because it is exuding from their child, and therefore the parents are also connecting with this immense energy.

If new-borns are fortunate enough to arrive into a healthy, well-adjusted family, this one hundred percent of love is allowed to stay. A healthy childhood equates to keeping this full one hundred percent of pure love, and further continuous reiteration equates to high self-esteem, high self-worth, and high self-respect, which creates personal boundaries and therefore learns to prioritise oneself.

Unfortunately, if the parents have unresolved issues and so, therefore, have their own agenda, the child becomes the focus of their own attempted healing and not in a healthy way either. Unhealthy treatment from parents, primary caregivers, and any perpetrator equate to a further reduction of this pure love.

So, to chart this information I have devised the following to show a possible reduction in self-love, self-worth, self-esteem, and self-respect as a result of this mistreatment.

Born: as one hundred percent of pure love.

Neglect in infancy: Loss of ten percent of pure love.

Now, at only ninety percent of pure love.

Mistreatment in the toddler stage: Loss of ten percent of pure love.

Now, at only eighty percent of pure love.

Physical/Emotional abuse at school age: Loss of ten percent of pure love.

Now, at only seventy percent of pure love.

Reiteration of low self-worth from parents/teachers/peers = Loss of ten percent of pure love.

Now, at only sixty percent of pure love.

Lack of support: Loss of ten percent of pure love.

Now, at only fifty percent of pure love.

Becoming aware of the reduction of love: Loss of ten percent of pure love.

Now at only forty percent of pure love.

Feeling pain connected to the loss of love: Loss of ten percent of pure love.

Now, at only thirty percent of pure love.

Confusion about what is right or wrong causes acceptance of repeated behaviour/information in childhood as being correct. Also, any lack of clarification of healthy behaviour, due to neglect or emotional distancing, causes negative thoughts in adulthood when confronted with alternative healthy actions or behaviour from others. This present confusion then, is the cause of stress, depression, and anxiety, due to the continuous resurfacing and suppressing of uncomfortable emotions.

People possibly now begin to use denial, avoidance, and other defence mechanisms, so as not to feel this pain I.e., alcohol, drugs, overworking, and prioritising family, although these fixes are only temporary! In the absence of work, company, and activity, the painful truth is present in their thoughts and so the pain returns.

This is generally when the physical symptoms, as mentioned earlier, present themselves.

When choosing to participate in any talking therapy, there is a need for the client to identify that the situation usually gets worse before it gets better, and this is due to finally becoming aware of and no longer denying its existence! Also, beginning to refrain from using avoidance and defence mechanisms as a survival mechanism. So, this itself brings a further loss of pure love.

Now, of course, pure love is only twenty percent of pure love.

Self-reflection and exploration are also painful, so again a further ten percent loss of pure love is experienced.

The person now possibly only has an extreme low of ten percent of pure love.

The beginning of the healing journey includes acknowledgement and acceptance of lack of pure love from the external (parents and primary caregivers) although you do have the power to replenish this love from the internal, connecting to the source of this love, and choosing to receive what has been lost. Promoting self-love, which cannot be manipulated, reduced, or obliterated. Making time for yourself to explore and express, understand, and accept, that you are entitled to be again one hundred percent of pure love, and acknowledge that you can give this back to yourself because you have the power and capability to replenish what you are worthy of and entitled to, is your divine right.

Section Two
Mental

Mental health, these two words evoke such discomfort in some people.

A dictionary definition quotes these words as referring to: *'A person's condition with regard to their psychological and emotional well-being.'*

Although I would disagree! Which is another reason I have chosen to separate this book into four sections. I identify that psychological issues (mental – thinking) belong to cognitive issues, and emotional (symptoms) such as crying and screaming belong in their own category (emotional).

Yes, 'feelings' such as anger, sadness, fear, and happiness are our mental experiences of body states, but the emotional symptoms that arise as a result of these feelings are our responses to these feelings.

So, we are going to take a look at how we think and how that thinking process makes us feel in this section, and in section three we take a look at how these feelings cause us to react (emotionally).

Therefore, 'mental health' can be looked upon simply as how we 'think' and 'feel', separate from how we 'act' (as a result of any unpleasant thoughts and feelings).

If we look to the word control and take a few moments to reflect on it. If you feel in control of your own life, your own future, your own thoughts, your own feelings, or your own actions? At what point did you decide you lacked control?

Not feeling in control of life, in general, would certainly cause great anguish. Yet why should people be embarrassed because they have temporarily lost control of their own lives? When in fact, the real embarrassment should belong to whatever or whoever took control away from this person.

There are many people who unfortunately are experiencing unresolved historic issues and the only way they can make themselves feel better is to exert control over someone or something else, whether that be in a position of power in a workplace, control over an animal, control over their partner, or control over their own children.

People either deal with their issues externally, making themselves feel temporary relief from their own pain by projecting it onto others or struggle with their issues internally, resulting in self-sabotage physically or mentally. This could include physical self-harm, self-medication (drink or drugs) or simply by berating themselves (defined as: 'To scold or condemn in a forceful or intense manner; with great feeling and at length').

Those people who inflict suffering on others may be classified as possible Manipulators, Narcissists, Sociopaths or even Psychopaths, and all are experiencing mental health problems. This is because they do not feel any remorse or guilt connected to their behaviour. Whereas people who find themselves on the receiving end of this behaviour would fall into a category of having difficulty with their 'emotional health' (brought about by experiencing a volatile situation).

Sometimes changing this situation can begin the healing by removing themselves from it, although this is not always possible. Therefore, coping strategies could be explored.

Having no conscience or remorse could be identified as experiencing mental health issues, but feeling vulnerable, afraid, or unhappy could be identified as experiencing emotional issues. Maybe, just maybe, this could reduce this stigma, although better still any stigma could be obliterated totally.

To associate the mental element connected to our brain garden, I would identify the connection as being the water (or rain) that feeds and nourishes the weeds, allowing them to stay alive, thrive and even cause overgrowth.

Although the original weeds were planted by external negative messages, the mistaken beliefs then derived from the receipt of these causes reiteration, and so these weeds have now been nourished, causing them to thrive and remain steadfast. You have to take ownership over your own thoughts, you are not a puppet, although you have possibly felt like you are, and each time you allow a mistaken belief to take up space in your head you are watering these weeds.

A mistaken belief is someone having taken ownership of a negative message, and although people will attempt to tell a false truth, to undermine them in an attempt to break their spirit and gain control if a person is full of self-love these words will have no impact. Although unfortunately, for someone who has experienced an unhealthy or volatile childhood, these false truths will trigger pain in an unresolved wound, and due to the soreness of this wound and the weakness they feel as a result of this, they will find it difficult to defend themselves. These projected words then connect with and reiterate those who already heard negative messages and now become mistaken beliefs.

So, the water you pour onto these weeds by absorbing these messages will keep them healthy and thriving, until such time as you explore and resolve your pain, and so uproot these weeds.

If someone has ever felt themselves to be like a puppet, meaning they have not felt in control of their own thoughts and decisions: not only in childhood but continuing into adulthood also, then when they are put into an adult situation, like a work role for instance, where the puppeteer is absent, this is where anxiety can take control! This person is now left up to their own devices, but not having been in this position of responsibility before they, unfortunately, do not have a clue how to deal with it, and if after they have been given responsibility in this role, mistakes are made within this environment, therefore, this would only serve as yet more reiteration of their low opinion of themselves. Trust in themselves is non-existent in their ability to achieve even simple tasks, and so to compensate for this lack of trust they repeat the task again and again and again, and yes you have now probably recognised the pattern of Obsessive-Compulsive Disorder (OCD).

In the author's opinion, through observation and treatment, people who experience OCD (and I refrain from using the word 'suffer' deliberately!) do so sometimes as a result of a complete lack of trust in themselves, to accomplish a task correctly and to keep others (and themselves) safe. They keep searching for completion and collaboration, although it is never forthcoming because they have never been able to learn to trust themselves, because in childhood they lacked control, due to all decisions and responsibilities never having been allocated to them. (This is generally performed in an age-appropriate manner).

OCD can also arise in adulthood possibly due to wrong decision-making and the ensuing results, causing the trust they already had, to be lost.

This constant reiteration of repeated failed attempts to carry out and achieve simple tasks (of counting, locking doors, turning off ovens etc) only serves to cause an overgrowth of weeds in their brain garden, and so it has now become what resembles a forest, with this person identifying that any possible thought of cultivation impossible, and yet it is not impossible.

Trust in oneself is a mental state, you either trust yourself or you do not, you have learned to trust yourself or you have not (or you have lost trust in yourself). OCD is not an identity, it does not define a person, and it is not a character trait! It is a phase, however long that phase has lasted it is still a phase, it was not present at birth, it is a learned behaviour, due to not learning (or losing) something else, trust! So, a person can learn or relearn this.

After discussing the above information with a client, I introduced what I called, a *self-chit,* (or self-receipt) book into the mix, this was a tiny A7 size notebook with a tiny pen attached which could be carried in a pocket, on the first page of this notepad was five words namely: Action, Date, Time and Signed.

My client on completing an OCD task would then jot down the:

Action: i.e., turn off the cooker.

Date: That day's date.

Time: The time the action was completed.

Signed: And then my client would sign or initial that the task had been completed.

When my client had a compulsion to repeat the task, this client would check their 'self-chit' notepad and see if this task had already been carried out. At the beginning of this exercise, the client still felt a need to check again, although the agreement was that each time a check was made another chit had to be written out.

Eventually, this client began to build up trust in themselves the fact that they alone had indeed completed this and other tasks to their own acceptance level, accept, until such time that there was no need to re-check the task and no need for the self-chit book. The time it took to achieve this was minimal in comparison to the fact that some people have experienced OCD for decades.

So even when your brain garden feels completely unmanageable, there is still hope! And as having hope is another mental state, one's attitude toward change is key!

Feeling overwhelmed can lead to experiencing depression as well as anxiety and finding yourself in an environment where there is a need to take responsibility, however minimal, can escalate this. This overwhelm can also increase the amount of negative weeds, and this is as a result of the quantity of stress, rather than specifics.

Although, because a by others in childhood, this does not mean they are a failure! All things can be learned, and this includes trust in oneself, in addition to hope and faith.

In fact, to say we learn to trust ourselves in childhood through being given opportunity is not actually correct, we already instinctively trust ourselves from birth! This is why babies are not afraid to attempt new things, in respect of discovery. What babies are actually able to learn is 'a proof of their own trust in themselves', if they are given the opportunity to! Not being given these opportunities in the physical causes our spiritual instinctive knowing to deteriorate, and so then a dependency on the external (Parents) is created by the parents, to only trust in what they trust in.

When babies are born, they are fully equipped with survival instincts, to be kept warm and fed and to receive these survival needs they draw attention to themselves by crying. They are not upset; they are creating attention to get their needs met, although if these needs are ignored, then they become upset! This is why crying babies do not always have tears because, initially, their crying is simply an attempt at communication.

If babies lived without parents and therefore did not absorb their parent's rules and opinions their characters would be so different of course, which is why all children are different! Because they are a reflection of their parent's rules, opinions, and regulations. Although this responsibility is not solely with the parents, physically it is yes, (the need for food and warmth) but spiritually ('a belief in oneself' for reiteration), mentally and emotionally, a baby has its own inherent coping strategies, and these originally derive whence it came via creation: biological and genetical.

So, for parents to consider that they have the ultimate responsibility for their baby's growth and welfare is quite ignorant of the concept of evolution.

A baby born in the present has more capabilities than a baby born to a Neanderthal, who were the subspecies of modern humans, and modern humans have a more evolved brain at birth. If parents focussed their attention on their responsibilities surrounding the physical needs of their baby and focussed less responsibility on their emotional and mental welfare, maybe there would be fewer mentally and emotionally damaged adults?

Therapy is not always about mentally learning new things; it is sometimes about unlearning things that should not have been taught by parents. Raising a well-adjusted child is a huge responsibility and for parents to identify that they simply know how to is a poor judgement. Maternal and paternal emotions toward a baby, of kindness and protectiveness, are awesome, although a baby's brains are empty vessels waiting to absorb cognitive information like a sponge. Unfortunately, babies do not have a brain filter capability, so their brain absorbs ALL information, whether positive or negative! And they also do not have the capability to sift through and discard any unhelpful learning.

I shall refer back to the analogy of the laptop I used earlier, in the respect of it being your parents who originally owned this laptop and so downloaded all of its present files. Some files could be correct although some could also be incorrect, some files could be useful but then some files could be useless, also, unfortunately, some files could contain a virus, causing any healthy files to be contaminated. So, the same as what you would do with that laptop when you do a factory reset, you can do it yourself and do a birth reset! To perform a deep clean and become the person you were meant to be before any incorrect input caused your present-day thinking.

As an adult, you do have a filter system and so you can sift through each thought and memory, view it, reflect on it then decide whether to keep or delete it! This is now your responsibility, your choice, and your decision.

As adults, we are also able to look to parents as individuals in their own right, not simply as parents to agree with and obey, and as you would disagree with some opinions of your partner, friend, or colleague, you are now also able to disagree with the opinions of your parents! And just because they are your parents this does not make them right. You can still respect and have contact with your parents whilst disagreeing with their opinions, rules, and regulations, or you can choose to go 'no contact'. This is your decision. Some people choose to sever all ties completely, some choose reduced contact, and some choose minimal contact, but ultimately this decision has to be based on your health needs and not the needs of your parents.

Misplaced loyalty can be a barrier when deciding to prioritise you in respect of relationships with parents, although this has a lot to do with social constructs. The pressure from the retail sector to celebrate and embrace relations with parents who use quotations such as 'A Mother is an angel sent from heaven' or 'A Mother is your best friend' etc and yet we have all possibly come across someone in our childhood who is struggling with their own issues and so are projecting their venom on others, and these people grow up to become parents! But this does not automatically mean they become saint-like or angelic at the birth of their baby! So, create personal boundaries when entering card shops, do not absorb the pressure to conform and think of all parents as people who should be praised and put on a pedestal, because unfortunately, some are not, and you now as an adult have the power to choose your own thoughts and decisions regarding your feelings towards, and your relationship with your parents.

Some parents choose to use their children to give them identity, and so they identify the thought of losing their children as also losing their identity, although their children are only loaned to them until adulthood when they become their own person. The saying 'You will always be my baby boy/girl' is not endearing; this is only about the parent and is unfair to their child. Of course, their children will always be their son or daughter, but they will not always be a, or their baby. Parenting is not about having children be dependent on parents; it is about teaching children to become independent. Children should be allowed to grow and flee the nest when the time comes, and if they return that is because they want to, and not derived from a sense of duty or responsibility. So, to say to a child you will always be my…etc. is clipping their wings of independence and freedom. As a child, connect to your right to fly, and as a parent respect your child's right of flight.

The saying, 'You only have one mother', or father of course, can amount to huge feelings of guilt when you are contemplating reducing contact, although you may have even heard this from a mother who still expects respect after mistreating their child! So again, 'observe don't absorb' because this is about them projecting their own issues onto you. And, if we explore this from a spiritual angle: then you may only have one biological/physical mother in this physical realm, but we are given the information that all of us have spiritual parents in a different realm who can provide us with unconditional abundant love if we open ourselves up to this possibility and awareness.

Even though you can choose to distance yourself physically from your parents (or an abusive partner) mentally and emotionally, you will still be attached, until such time as you do your brain reset, and prune all those negative weeds. Although sometimes try as you might, you may still find that you cannot detach from these people no matter what you do! Now, this could be as a result of you holding on to unhealthy thoughts such as anger or resentment, and this is about you, not them!

Forgiveness is the only way to release this mental and emotional attachment, and yes, I can hear you say, 'No way will I ever forgive that person who hurt me,' but forgiving someone does not mean you ever forget what they did, because you cannot, and although it could become a distant memory, it will no doubt be triggered at some inopportune moment, causing you to feel angry or upset unless you have dealt with it. So, dealing with it means exploring the possibility of forgiveness.

This is not about interacting with the perpetrator or having any communication with him/her whatsoever, what this means is simply changing your mindset by changing your thoughts. Each time you think of this person and you possibly get an uncomfortable feeling in the pit of your stomach, which is unpleasant to you, this is anger! So, all you need to do at this point is introduce mindfulness and say to yourself, 'I choose to let go of this anger', say it again and again until this discomfort subsides, or until your attention has been diverted onto another situation. At this moment, your focus is not on what that person did to you, so you are not holding onto that anger, your focus is on your wellbeing and your comfort. The anger is losing its strength, it is dispersing and weakening, and so you are is in control at this moment, of your thoughts, of your discomfort and of your future. Anger and unforgiveness is a mental state, either a choice or a decision, and so to regain control is to release these emotions that originated connected to the perpetrator. Therefore, for as long as you are connected to them, the longer you are also connected to the perpetrator. So, take back control and choose forgiveness.

After all, forgiveness is simply letting go of the hurtful memories and the hold that the anger has on you!

In respect of 'messages we receive' as children from primary caregivers or others, we have to identify both direct and also indirect, as up until this point we have focussed only on direct messages i.e., insults or criticisms, although indirect messages are received simply as a result of observation.

Should a child be born into a family where domestic violence is prevalent and therefore has to witness these happening on a daily basis (whether that be verbal or physical) the children of the family being exposed to this, will as a result portray symptoms of PTSD. An experience such as this will have the same effect on a child as a soldier experiencing combat in battle. Experiencing aggression and violence impacts a child's brain in the same magnitude and so will affect their general behaviour and also their general outlook on life. Thoughts connected to adults, their environment; also, the world, in general, will be greatly impacted, resulting in a sense of hopelessness and also difficulty in forming or maintaining close relationships. Unfortunately, these children will develop trauma-specific fears, manifesting possibly as lack of trust in either or all genders, in addition to displaying anger tantrums, experiencing nightmares and also changes in behaviour such as bedwetting or sucking their thumb (Terr, 1991).

If this behaviour or the symptoms are not addressed, the effect of experiencing just one or a multitude of domestic violence incidents will continue into adulthood, and so this underlying feeling of fear or panic could, unfortunately, evolve into anxiety and/or depression. All too often lack of resolve from external sources due to deficiency of acknowledgement or understanding will result in those that have experienced these traumas to self-medicate, and so turn to alcohol or drugs in an attempt to subdue their pain or what they consider to be their weakness.

Sometimes people need the help of a professional to help them return to inner peace and as Psychodynamic therapy allows for exploration of an individual's childhood a therapist is, therefore, able to identify and address childhood traumas, which can, in turn, lead to resolve, and healing. Although the individual does need to 'want' to be healed initially for the outcome to be successful. Prior to healing, struggles that the now-adult will experience would be on a wide spectrum possibly including OCD, Anorexia, Bulimia Nervosa, also self-harming to name a few. Less obvious connected symptoms could include stuttering, skin conditions and possibly various phobias.

It may appear on the surface that the now-adult has dealt with or come to terms with the negative experiences endured in childhood to others and also themselves, and so they may be confused as to why they are experiencing 'poor mental health' in their present day. Although simply because the cause of their condition is no longer a regular occurrence due to their parent's possible death or divorce, below the surface the symptoms of their experiences are still active. Just like a physically open wound that has become infected, if not treated, a scab will form at the opening giving the appearance of healing, whilst the actual wound becomes more festered by the day through lack of attention and treatment.

This form of therapy endeavours to remove that scab, during the exploration of childhood memories, which can of course be painful, but this is in order to reach the infection (or bad energy), and in doing so healing of the cause can begin.

Unfortunately, some people who accept outside help are only prepared to disclose to their therapist surface issues, similar to showing them a bandaged wound, although in order to heal the bandage must be removed to reveal the scabbed over the wound, at this point the air will allow the healing to happen quicker, similar to exposure and exploration of suppressed hurts allowing that healing to begin.

It takes courage to bare your soul to a stranger although Carl Rogers (1957) a pioneer of Person-Centred Counselling advised that initially, the therapist shall create the conditions for change for the client, in that the counsellor should be warm, genuine, and understanding. It is considered an equal partnership, in which the therapist is aiding the client to find their solutions and is therefore empowering for the client. Given The underlying basis for person-centred counselling is self-actualisation Carl Rogers believed that all things have a tendency to reach their full potential even if their present situation or circumstances have prevented any further development. He derived that given the correct conditions, every organism, whether human or vegetable will thrive to attain its full growth, therefore it is only their living conditions which are conditioned out of their control, so will then prevent anything from realising its true worth.

He also suggested that in order for a counsellor to be truly at one with the client and for the client to be able to grow spiritually and emotionally, the counsellor had to possess certain attributes; he called these 'Core Conditions'. If these conditions were present in the counsellor's qualities and attitude this will enable the client to relax and so make exceptional progress. These Core Conditions are: Empathy, Congruence and Unconditional Positive Regard (UPR).

To explain further, having empathy with a person is having the ability to see the world through the other person's eyes and from their frame of mind, to be able to feel exactly how they are feeling within their frame of reference and so recognising their distress and therefore being able to have complete understanding.

In order for a counsellor to be congruent with a client, the counsellor has to possess the ability to be very genuine. Firstly, by being open and honest with themselves about their own thoughts and feelings in reference to their own experiences, then, in turn, allowing them to portray the same in their understanding and response to the client's own issues and dilemmas. Being congruent breaks down any barriers of lack of communication due to thoughts of superiority, ignorance, or denial and so this then allows for unprejudiced awareness, bringing harmony and unity to the counsellor-client relationship. And finally, being able to give unconditional positive regard is the ability to be non-judgmental to a client's standing or situation, being able to accept them as they are with all or any flaws and/or behaviour issues. A therapist who utilises the person-centred theory and has this attribute is able to transcend all boundaries of predisposed thoughts and opinions with each and every client, and therefore is able to deal with all in the same manner of valuing their individual humanity.

And so, if a therapist has learning in both the Person-Centred and the Psychodynamic theories, the journey into a painful childhood need not be so daunting.

Explaining PTSD further the author chooses to liken it to, *Decompression sickness* (also known as *the bends* or *caisson disease*) in the respect that: deep-sea divers experiencing extreme pressure also aviators experiencing high altitude, afterwards have to submit to a decompression chamber in order to avoid this condition. In the event such people do not partake in decompression unfortunately they will experience the results of such, which involves bubbles growing in tissue and causing local damage, this, in turn, causes various symptoms including dizziness and weakness, joint aches or pains, tremors, and shakes, also numbness (Thalmann, 2004).

So, if a person has unfortunately experienced a traumatic event and this has not been addressed also, this person is still expected to function normally in daily life, this in itself will result in him/her experiencing debilitating symptoms. Furthermore if this continues not to be addressed the situation and symptoms can worsen over time. Although had this debility been acknowledged and treated at the time, the ensuing months or years of poor mental health could have been avoided.

To expand even further on PTSD let us identify that being involved in normal day to day activities at a steady pace, the brain has the capability of processing all of the included information adequately, although if unfortunately, someone experiences a traumatic event, the part of our brain that is concerned with survival (known as the reptilian brain, due to it being the most primitive part and is located to the back and base of the skull) kicks into action like a fire alarm being activated when smoke has been detected, in order to offer protection. The primary responsibility of this part of the brain is to identify if we can FIGHT this threat? Can we FLIGHT (away from this threat)? Or do we FREEZE i.e., remain silent and hide until the threat has passed?

So, although this part of the brain has our best interest at heart the problem is once this usually dormant part has been activated there is no natural way to deactivate it! This then causes the person to feel they are still living with this threat to their safety long after the incident has passed. The person is now in a constant state of arousal, on constant high alert, aware of detecting any and all threats, even though none exists in their current circumstances. One way to counteract this overdrive and to silence the persistent reiterations of needing to protect themselves is to introduce the mantra 'I AM SAFE' persistently, whenever able to. This is making use of Neuroplasticity and creating a neural pathway with this new information.

Flashbacks experienced as a result of PTSD are the fragmented memories of the traumatic incident, liken it if you will to a jigsaw that has been strewn across a floor, all the pieces are there although they are not connected (processed). In order to process these memories correctly so that they can be filed away in the brain like any other less traumatic experience, revisiting the memories of the traumatic event allows for these scattered memories to become in alignment. Although this is best done with a professional who will explore and prompt the client to not allow any segment of memory (or piece of jigsaw) to be missed.

Trauma is at the root of many mental health struggles, although not every negative experience is identified as trauma. The traumatic experience itself may have a totally different effect on two individuals, and the reason for this is dependent on what each person is currently dealing with in their everyday life, or, in fact, if they have historic unresolved issues. Although PTSD is quite simply a normal response to overwhelming events. To take things at face value can be very detrimental to a person's mental wellbeing as symptoms are not always visible. Lack of acknowledgement can cause the person involved to internalise their emotions thinking themselves personally weak, although even simple recognition of the effects a traumatic experience can have on a person's mental health can go a long way in avoiding poor mental health long term.

Another recognition, which would be beneficial to the sufferer would be for all medical professionals to acknowledge the mind-body connection and the negative energy of the trauma which can get trapped in the mind and body, causing various symptoms until such times as it is released via therapy. Shamans, who are healers with Native American heritage identify that this negative energy can be released by means of meditation, and having a Shaman going into a deep trance which they describe as 'journeying' in order to retrieve an element of the person's soul which had become detached or lost as a result of experiencing trauma. This is known as soul retrieval and interestingly, some people experiencing depression often describe themselves as feeling 'lost'.

Shamans recognise that all mental health issues are connected to spiritual disturbances, which can manifest as physical symptoms if not treated, hence the mind-body connection.

So far, we have focussed on what did happen in childhood, although issues can arise as a result of what did not happen! As we have identified, babies are born as empty vessels, which can be filled with either positive or negative messages as a result of observation or direct interaction. Although the responsibility of parents is also to teach their children how to deal with or cope with life.

In general, people can 'plod on' with life provided they are not presented with problems, but when a problem does arise as a result of experiencing death, redundancy, divorce, work-related stress etc, they can identify that they are unable to cope. Instantly, people will view this inability to cope as a negative mark on their personality, in turn, which could manifest into self-sabotage, including self-criticism and also self-harm. Yet this is not an inability to cope due to being inadequate, this is an inability to cope due to not being taught coping mechanisms in childhood! Generally, because parents were also not taught how to! But how can we expect ourselves to simply know how to do anything if we have not been taught? We are shown and so learn how to drive a car, we are shown and so we learn how to cook, we are shown and so learn how to read and write, etc. We cannot expect ourselves to know how to do anything unless we have been shown how to!

And so, the key here is to initially reduce the expectations we place on ourselves, take a step back and instead accept that we have to learn this ability!

This is not as difficult as it sounds, it feels difficult initially because we are still beating ourselves up due to our inadequacy, but once we drop that beating stick to the ground, already we connect to reprieve and so feel less traumatised. We can then move on accepting that we simply were not taught this attribute in childhood and allow it to resonate that all things can be learned.

Here we can connect again with neuroplasticity, and a negative neural pathway that has been created because of a self-inflicted negative message would possibly be 'I can't do this' or 'I can't cope with this' because we know no difference at this point! And although this feels like a fact in the pit of your stomach, this is only a mistaken belief. Therefore, you need to replace that incorrect acceptance with the correct information of 'I CAN DO THIS' and 'I CAN COPE'. Of course, the already established negative neural pathway will keep firing and trying to correct you, because our brain at that moment knows no difference until we teach it so. You have to ride with those thoughts whilst you are attempting to change them, and no, it is not easy! You will feel like you are pushing against a brick wall, but that is exactly what you are doing. Although in connecting to your inner strength and dedicating yourself to this change, with determination and persistence you will achieve this change! It is not that you cannot cope, it is because you never learned how to, so this is not inadequacy, this is simply you returning to a lesson that you missed out on. Another thing to recognise though is that when we are involved in a healing journey, we do not need to look to point a finger or lay any blame, although we do have to identify where our struggles originate, this is just to give us an insight and an understanding. To accept that parents were neglectful in some parental responsibilities is also accepting that they knew no difference, as they too were not taught how, and so, they did the best job that they knew how to do.

As babies, we assign meanings to first time experiences, so then, if the child receives validation for these assumptions, by way of their repetitive behaviour, mistaken beliefs are then gained from this incorrect information. For instance, if a child is not taught – to not touch ornaments in their own home, then when in someone else's home and because they have the belief that it is okay to touch ornaments, they will do so. The child is not doing wrong in his/her eyes, so they will become confused and frustrated, wondering why he/she is not being allowed to touch them, the same applies to all new experiences, and the responses received. All-day, everyday learning is taking place: What is right, what is wrong and what is acceptable behaviour and what is not? It is not always direct messaging though, neglect plays a huge part in building a baby's beliefs because their assumptions are not being dismissed, and therefore they give their incorrect belief simply by not being shown otherwise.

Each time they behave in the same way, and each time they are not told differently, this repetitive behaviour from parents creates a 'this behaviour is okay' anchor in the child, although anchors can also be created by an emotional attachment to a single situation.

If an achievement is gained and this is not recognised or celebrated, from learning to walk to possibly winning an egg and spoon race in infancy, the response the child receives will create their self-worth, they learn if they are worthy to be celebrated or not. This response from parents or primary caregivers will become an anchor, as it was an experience with an emotional attachment i.e., excited, happy etc and so the response was received during the same emotionally heightened state for the child, and so the anchor has been created. It is a huge responsibility to constantly be aware of reactions, although if a mistake is made, it can be rectified soon after by expressing acknowledgement and pride in the achievement.

If this does not happen or did not happen in childhood, all is not lost! Great emphasis is put upon external recognition, although self-recognition brings the same sense of self-worth, so it is just a matter of learning to self-praise. All the negativity surrounding: *It not being right to blow your own trumpet*, is a farce generated by people who struggle to do so! Hopefully, they too will learn how to someday, so any achievement or accomplishment you have succeeded in, you blow your own trumpet! Celebrate yourself by buying yourself a gift, looking at yourself in the mirror and saying out loud, 'WELL DONE YOU!' You deserve to and you are allowed to! So, begin by giving yourself permission to do so!

When people choose to reflect on their childhood and identify mistakes that were made it is a good thing to tell ourselves that our parents were possibly not taught parental skills by their own parents, so what they did know, was all they had to go on! Although you can break the chain, you can be a better parent to your child/ren and in turn, they too will be good parents to their offspring.

Unfortunately, people sometimes have their own insecurities and lack of trust in the world due to unpleasant experiences or neglect, so this then manifests onto their own children by way of creating unhealthy dependencies, this then causes children to have attachment issues and in turn prevents their children from becoming independent, well-adjusted adults. To love parents is good, to miss parents is okay, although to feel unable to live away from parents or constantly wanting to be in contact with them does not make way for growth, either emotionally, mentally, or spiritually. Sons and daughters of dependent parents experience anxiety at the thought of living apart from parents, although should their parents pass over before they do, then this is something they will experience. The very thought of that causes panic attacks, and yet this is all brought about by mistaken beliefs, that they could not cope or survive without being separated from them, yet they have never ever done it, so how do they know? So, you see some thoughts are not facts!

In CBT, there is an exercise entitled, *Systematic Desensitisation,* systematic meaning: A system is used to change behaviour, and desensitisation means to reduce the sensitivity attached to the situation. The approach to this exercise involves gradually introducing a client to the subject that they are fearful of, as this fear is possibly only present as a result of mistaken beliefs. For instance, a parent who was afraid of heights has taught their child (indirectly) to also be afraid of heights. Initially, this exercise would involve the client viewing pictures or photographs of views taken from a specific height until they felt comfortable to move on viewing pictures taken from a greater height. Once any anxiety connected with this is brought under control, the client would then be introduced to a physical height, and this height then being increased, at their own pace, again until the client was absent of any anxiety. During this exercise, the client is made to feel safe and secure, allowing them to build up trust in themselves.

Lack of trust in self is responsible for a multitude of anxiety issues and gradually building up this trust allows for a better quality of life, by being able to participate in things they were previously unable to.

Children have to be prepared for adulthood and this responsibility is not only on primary caregivers but also on biological factors. Adolescence can sometimes be seen as a troublesome time for parents, although if they had more knowledge of what is actually happening in the child's body at this time, there is a possibility that relations may not have to be so fraught. Andrew Curran (2008) explains that adolescence is a pre-programmed neurobiological event, with serotonin levels gradually increasing from childhood to adulthood, as with dopamine, on the same par. Although, between the ages of roughly thirteen and seventeen there is a huge dopamine surge! This is predetermined normal neurobiology, and all adolescents experience this! Until this high level returns to that of serotonin. The reason for this is because the body is getting children naturally ready for adulthood, and nature actually wants children to take high risks, with poor judgement! There are two reasons for this, firstly to instigate independence from parents, and secondly to connect with peers via trial and error in order to adjust to adulthood where they are expected to fend for themselves. It is also thought that during adolescence certain conditions are developed such as depression, autism, bipolar disorder, also addiction. We need our dopamine and serotonin levels to be regulated and this relies heavily on what we eat, what we do, and what we think (maintaining stress levels). Also, as dopamine production is connected to the emotional part of our brain, to receive love, but more so to connect with self-love which causes its activation, therefore love is the key!

Unfortunately, stress, alcohol, and drugs of addiction can give us too much of a dopamine surge, causing us not to be able to think or function correctly. Fortunately, though, increasing our serotonin can come to the rescue here, as it reduces the activation of nerve cells, and in doing so also reduces high dopamine levels.

So, you see what appears to be a mental attitude i.e., disrespectful, and argumentative can in fact be related to a biological condition, and if anyone who was ever labelled as a difficult child can disassociate from this label as it was not all their fault!

In order to increase serotonin by way of a positive mental attitude about yourself, it is identifying that you are not all that you were told you were, or that you were led to believe! You can identify your own positive description of yourself and create your own (mental) thoughts based on this description. You become what you believe, and so to change your thoughts change your beliefs, and as our thoughts cause a reaction in our body, you can either choose to become mentally and physically healthier or remain as you are. Negative thoughts about yourself directed inward are self-sabotaging, and experiments have been performed to identify the effect that negative words can have on cooked rice, by Dr Masaru Emoto, also the effect that aggressive or gentle music has on water.

These experiments demonstrate that projecting negative energy has a profound destructive effect. In his book, *The Hidden Messages In Water,* Dr Masaru Emoto explains this but also demonstrates his experiments on his YouTube channel. Everyone can choose to try out these experiments for themselves, and schools have even chosen to use these demonstrations to clarify how harmful bullying is. Try it out! You will be amazed.

When children reach adolescence, and if they have ever objected or disagreed with their parent's choices previously (and have been dismissed or rejected), this is the time where they become even more adamant in their objections, resulting in possible volatile relationships. Although still living with parents and having to follow guidelines, it is difficult for children to be assertive and attempt to pursue their own ideas. Children have their own personalities, and until adulthood and independence, they sometimes have to suppress this, so it is beneficial to understand this concept and to connect with their frustrations.

As the poet Kahlil Gibran (1883–1931) puts it:

Your children are not your children.
They are sons and daughters of life's longing for itself.
They come through you but not from you.
And though they are with you,
Yet they belong not to you.
You may give them your love, but not your thoughts,
For they have their own thoughts.
You may house their bodies, but not their souls,
For their souls dwell in the house of tomorrow,
Which you cannot visit, not even in your dreams.
You may strive to be like them,
But seek not to make them like you.
For life goes not backward nor tarries with yesterday.

You are the bows from which your children as living arrows are sent forth.

The archer sees the make upon the path of the infinite,
And he bends you with his might,
That his arrows may go swift and far.
Let your bending in the archer's hand be for gladness.
For even as he loves the arrow that flies,
So, he also loves the bow that is stable.

Parents who identify that they struggled in their own childhood have to be aware of possibly projecting absorbed negative messages and mistaken beliefs onto their own children. Creating this awareness can only benefit the parent/child relationship.

Unhealthy mistaken beliefs can pass from generation to generation, never being questioned and with children simply conforming through neuroplasticity yet having a 'knowing' that something does not feel right.

It takes courage to stand up and bring attention to something that has been accepted as 'the norm' for many years, yet this courage will allow for the breaking of the chain of tradition. People hold on to tradition with tremendous loyalty, yet some ideas and opinions were generated for a world that no longer exists! We are constantly evolving physically, mentally, emotionally, and spiritually, and if you keep yourself strapped to the past, you will miss out on all that the present and the future have to offer.

Therefore, it is beneficial to be open to new ideas and pass these new ideas on to your own children, but also attempt to share these ideas with older relatives! Yes, you may be rebuffed but do not let that prevent you from embracing evolvement, as you were born into a different world to your parents, and your children were/will be born into a different world than you.

Everyone benefits from mindfulness meditation and fortunately, schools and colleges are introducing this into their curriculum (as are prisons also introducing this). Finally, it is beginning to be recognised that bad behaviour is not only about reprimanding but also about repairing. As self-spoken positive words can lift our spirits, so too can listening to recordings of positive affirmations, and also specific music. This music can have words included or be simply instrumental, although the important thing is to listen to the correct frequency.

Music is enormously powerful, so if you only listen to music that speaks of betrayal, sadness, or abandonment, all that will have a negative effect on your vibrational frequency. Therefore, uplifting words in songs is what you need to listen to, and if these are put together with a specific musical frequency this all assists in raising your vibration.

So, pay attention to the lyrics of the music you listen to, but also check on what frequency the music is being played at as it may be decreasing your vibrational frequency.

Knowledge is power, and all knowledge increases your mental capacity, so the more you know about how to make yourself feel better, the more personal power you will have.

Vibration in quantum physics means that 'everything is energy'. We are beings whose energy can vibrate at certain frequencies. Each vibration is equivalent to a feeling, and in the vibrational world; there are only two types of vibrations, positive and negative. Any feeling causes you to emit a vibrational frequency that can be positive or negative (Roupe,

2020). As our thoughts affect our feelings, we always have to remain mindful of the mental thoughts that we are having, which are always affecting our feelings!

I have put together a list of musical frequencies and how they relate to assisting in your wellbeing. And all these can be researched, downloaded, and listened to on YouTube:

528Hz Assists with DNA Repair.

432Hz Induces sleep.

417Hz Reduces symptoms of PTSD.

396Hz Allows grief to become more manageable.

741Hz Increases confidence.

852Hz Raises intuition.

963Hz Restores spiritual awareness.

Dr Lee Bartel promotes what he refers to as 'music medicine', and after years of research and experiments, he has identified that specific frequencies in music have a huge impact on the neurons in our brain, and that sound can stimulate cells in your body, as well as your brain. The advice he has given to an Alzheimer's sufferer is what he describes as a 'prescription'; to listen to a low frequency of 40 Hz for half an hour, three times a week, this resulted in brain stimulation from this vibrational frequency and in turn had a profound positive impact on her Alzheimer's condition, by restoring connectivity (Clements-Cortes et al., 2017). Similarly, to reduce the impact of Fibromyalgia pain, Alzheimer's disease, Parkinson's disease, depression, and even increase blood flow, he has created musical compilations which are available to purchase.

Your personal vibration is generated inside of you through your own personal choices, this is referred to as the 'home frequency' and if someone has wronged you and so lowers this frequency Peirce (2009) you then have a choice, to remain there or to project yourself upwards from those depths. Similar to being in deep water, to rise to the surface you have to rely on your own strength, although bringing about a change in your frequency simply relies on you going into relaxation and meditation, connecting the present moment, and choosing to no longer be connected to this negative vibrational frequency.

As this section of the book focuses on the mental element of our being, and our mental capability relies on our mental capacity, embracing an array of knowledge can only be beneficial. Even if you are sceptical about some of what you have read here, humour the author, and connect to the quote 'Don't knock it until you try it!' And even if you downright disagree, do it anyway! As results have occurred simply from people entertaining the possibility of a result. This is known as, *The Placebo Effect*.

This effect is defined as a phenomenon in which some people experience a benefit after the administration of an inactive 'look-alike' substance or treatment. Scientists have discovered that the placebo effect causes the brain to release more of a natural painkiller, and doctors have seen an improvement in a medical condition caused by a patient's belief as opposed to taking medication orally or receiving actual treatment.

So, if you choose to believe you will improve your mental health, you will! As you can simply tell yourself that you are improving, and your brain will act according to the information you are feeding it. When we have explored Neuroplasticity previously, well, this is just another element of Neuroscience.

The brain does not know the difference between fact and fiction, truth or false! It does not have eyes to see, or ears to hear! And as a deaf/blind person relies on being led too, the brain relies on being led. Therefore, we can manipulate the brain to our own advantage, we can tell it what we want, provided we tell it multiple times!

The brain cannot distinguish real from imaginary, and so if you are actually involved in a stressful situation or the situation has passed, and you are just remembering it, your brain will still react the same to your feelings! So, as you begin to feel stressed by the memory, the brain produces the same stress hormone as it did during the actual situation.

Researchers at the Karolinska Institute in Sweden showed that when a person imagined moving fingers or toes it activated the fingers and toes regions of the brain as if they really were moving their fingers or toes.

The 'piano study' is an excellent example of neuroscience. Researchers at Harvard University compared the brains of people playing a sequence of notes on a piano with the brains of people imagining playing the notes. The region of the brain connected to the finger muscles was found to have changed to the same degree in both groups of people, whether they struck the keys physically or mentally.

It is this phenomenon, that the brain processes imagery as if it were real, which allows sportspeople to benefit from visualisation practices, so if pianists and sports personnel can do it, so too can you! (Hamilton, 2019).

You just have to think about what you want to believe and achieve, and it will happen! You are far more powerful than you have ever been led to believe, in fact, you have probably never ever been informed or made aware of your personal abilities and have just identified that the 'knowledge is power' phase is based on academic learning. Although this is about personal power and having knowledge of that power, and of your own greatness, harnessing that knowledge is the key to your greatness.

Whatever you choose to do to bring about your own healing ultimately 'time' is of the utmost importance, time to focus on yourself, and time to think about yourself. When was the last time you asked yourself questions, if ever? What do you want? What do you need? What is it that makes you happy? What is it that makes you unhappy? Where do you feel you lack control in your life? Take a few moments to answer those questions, and you may be surprised by what you find.

This is your path into a journey of self-discovery when you concentrate on yourself (which is described as participating in self-reflection). Self-development then comes from deciding to change the things that do not resonate with you, and eventually, self-love comes from identifying that you are worthy of making these changes. You are worthy of this time, you are worthy of these thoughts, and you are worthy of self-love.

You are a child of the universe no less than the trees and the stars; you have a right to be here. (Taken from the poem 'Desiderata' by Max Ehrmann).

Unfortunately, some of what you have been told were to suit other people, and so some of what you are feeling is connected to not being able to do what is right for you. Take for instance, after the birth of a new baby, and the new mother, as nature intended, wants to have time to herself to bond with her child, yet she is overwhelmed by well-wishers wanting to see and hold her newborn. Feeling that she is wrong for wanting to be alone can cause the new mother to sink into a low mood, yet these are natural instincts, which she is not able to connect with. And the more attention she receives, the more her mood sinks. If she were given more time to herself to spend alone with her child, and if she had the control to decide when she was ready to have visitors, rather than other people deciding when to visit, maybe more new mothers could possibly avoid post-natal depression?

All too often people do what they think is expected of them from others, rather than do what they think (or intuitively know) what is best for themselves.

To prioritise is important for mental health, irrespective of upsetting other people.

If you have ever witnessed the birth of kittens or puppies and have seen how fiercely protective the new mothers seem to be of their new-borns yet consider for a moment that they are not simply aggressive for the sake of their protection, but ultimately for the sake of their own bonding time. Humans are also entitled to this time, and it is for you to be assertive when deciding what is best for you.

Being in control of your own happiness means being in control of your own mental health, which means being in control of your own happiness! And taking control by prioritising yourself, means promoting self-love!

This is something you can teach yourself by encouragement, by nurturing, and by eventually building up trust in yourself, that you will take care of yourself in the future. In doing this you will be reversing the self-betrayal that people can feel as a result of letting themselves down, by not taking care of themselves up until now. Like a child learning to walk he/she is building up trust in the person who is teaching them, but also in him/herself, that they can achieve this frightening task. Life is the same in some respects, you have to take it one step at a time, and you will fall down, and maybe even feel hurt, but like that child, you can think you are safe when doing difficult tasks because you become aware that you have your own best interests at heart, and you allow yourself to get back up again.

Healing is not an incline, it comes with peaks and troughs (good days and bad days), although eventually the peaks will become more frequent than the troughs, and it takes time and attention from you.

Dedication, commitment, and repetition, putting as much effort into yourself as you put into looking after children, in your work role, or in your relationships is what will bring about results, and how quickly you see results of course depends on how much dedication, commitment and repetition you invest in yourself.

The children's nursery rhyme 'the three little pigs' comes to mind here, the first pig's house was built with straw (minimum effort) so could not withstand the force of the wolf blowing it down, the second pig's house was built using sticks (mediocre effort) and although the wolf had to try harder to blow it down, this house still could not avoid destruction, although the third pig's house which was built with bricks (maximum effort) was able to stay standing. The epilogue to this is: the more you want to get out of something the more effort you have to put in.

Even at the beginning of a healing journey, and even though you do not believe that you are worthy, you do the work anyway, because eventually, you will.

That third little pig could only see bricks and mortar but had faith that one day he would see a house, he had faith in himself, and so connecting to that faith in yourself, that you want to see change, and that you want to bring about this change, is the first step.

You could choose to be like the first pig, a victim of the wolf, or the second pig, a survivor (if only for a little longer than the first pig) or the third pig, a thriver , because he would then even be able to decorate his home! He had trust and faith in himself and in what he built for himself. (All pigs were eventually safe of course, but only by the first two relying on someone else). To become a thriver is ultimately about taking ownership and responsibility.

Everyone has a choice! To no longer be a victim of their experiences or circumstances, they can choose to become a survivor, and finally a thriver.

One way to think about a healing journey is to consider growing from a place of victimisation to survival, and then eventually to thriving, and although someone had no choice about being victimised, they do have a choice about evolving through these stages. Irrespective of a person's past, with understanding and acceptance of self, everyone can move through these stages and move beyond a time and experience of either a singular trauma or consistent traumatic interactions.

You may not have written the past, but you can become the author of your future, and you can create a new self-image. This could even involve writing a journal with the first page outlining the changes you want to implement. A journal has even been described as 'an outlet for despair' and so you could choose to decide to write any 'no send' letters in this journal, or simply express the anger and frustration of your thoughts onto the pages, but whatever you choose to do, deciding not to suppress unhealthy emotions any longer, is another step on the path to healing (Baikie and Wilhelm, 2005).

We can choose to change our thoughts, which in turn can change our attitude, for instance, if you feel anger towards someone who you feel has wronged you, for as long as you are carrying around this anger that person can trigger that anger. They do not even have to say anything; simply being in their presence will make you feel uncomfortable. Your mental ability will be in control at that moment, reliving whatever it was that they did to upset you, in your mind, and so your attitude will be negative toward that person. And yet you can change your attitude by deciding in that present moment that their presence will not and will never again cause you to feel upset. You can create a boundary of 'you don't affect me anymore', or 'you don't bother me anymore', you can recite this mantra to yourself all the time that you are in close proximity. We are capable of multitasking so even if your conscious mind is occupied with doing one thing, possibly on automatic pilot, your subconscious mind is occupied with sending a new message to your brain. And this subconscious part of your mind is actually the area you need to connect to!

Identify repetition as a conveyor belt, so the more you do something the more the first one gets put in the background, and our conscience's background is our subconscious!

The more that you do this; the more you are changing your attitude towards this person. This does not mean you are overlooking their behaviour, because you now have an awareness that you need to have boundaries around this person in respect of any present or future interactions, and if you work alongside this person so need to see them on a daily basis, what you are doing by changing your attitude toward them is making your day more pleasant for you!

Choosing to embrace this positive mental attitude is liberating because no longer does that person have control over your emotions, you do, and as inner peace is all about having complete control over our emotions, you will be well on your way to reaching this by beginning with dismissing any negative effect that anyone has on your mood.

You could even decide to write about this interaction (or person) in your journal on your return from your work (or outing). Express your anger and frustration onto the pages, let it flow; do not hold back, you are allowed to connect with all of your emotions, even anger, so you should not deny yourself feeling this. This is controlled anger, which is healthy, only when people suppress anger and then it erupts at inopportune moments or is directed at an innocent, is it inappropriate.

You could even decide to release this by screaming or shouting into a pillow! You could even decide to do both! Although if you have decided to express this anger onto paper, you can then choose to rip this section of your journal up into tiny pieces, and then either simply discard it into the waste, or choose to burn it in a suitable container. This act is considered another way of releasing negative energies.

Allowing yourself to participate in this also has a liberating effect on your mood, although you will not know this feeling unless you have participated in liberating exercises.

If the person who you feel has wronged you was once a friend, one way to view this is by identifying that life is like a delicious cream and sponge cake! As we grow, we are gathering the ingredients together, like plans of how we would like our future to be, we then bring together all the ingredients, the people we become friends with, family, the home we live in, the area where we live, etc, this then becomes our way of life, but if one piece of the cake (one part of your life) turns out to be unpleasant, (i.e., someone's piece turns out to have a hair in it! YUK!) That does not necessarily mean that the remaining sections have been tainted. You still have the goodness and sweetness of what is left, and so you can choose to focus your thoughts not on what has been damaged or lost, but that which you still have. This is living in gratitude. If you choose to, you could write a list of all the things that you have in your life, which you feel grateful for, and so exert your energies toward the pleasantries, which in turn will re-energise you, rather than toward what upsets you, which unfortunately depletes your energy.

Our thoughts affect our energy and those thoughts that were put there by others, if we continue to think negative thoughts; our energy continues to vibrate on a negative frequency. Although we can simply choose to think happy thoughts, this too raises our vibrational frequency.

Thoughts create our reality, whether that is a belief created from being given reiteration, or proof, or a belief from simply having faith in something or someone. Doctors, for instance, prescribing someone a tablet simply containing sugar (a placebo), patients have faith in the doctor that he knows what he/she is doing, but also faith in a cure from taking the medication that you have been given. Yet healing in this instance was what would have been accomplished by your own mind! Your thoughts, your mental capability! So, knowing this information, you can also begin to have faith in yourself!

Unfortunately, though, in addition to a placebo making you well it can also work in both ways and make you ill! We can even bring on illness! And this is known as, the *Nocebo effect*. Each unhealthy thought you have will be in effect giving you a dose of nocebo! Unfortunately, negative thoughts, especially about health, can even shut down our immune system (Dispenza, 2020).

Even if you have been fortunate enough to have lived a happy, healthy childhood but identify that you are struggling in the present day, which could be related to the world we live in at present.

Stress could be described as a state of mental or emotional tension or strain, which results from demanding or adverse situations or circumstances. As we have identified previously if you feel in control, you have inner peace, but with the demands placed on employees presently, including productivity, deadlines, and overall accomplishments, related to work, all of this amounts to work-related stress.

In addition, expectations from external factors such as parents, friends, work colleagues, partners, etc in connection to success, possessions, and achievements again all add to a feeling of being powerless over your own needs and wants, and instead, there is pressure to fulfil everyone else's needs and wants.

Pressure to perform, get results and produce expected outcomes, of course also amounts to stress, and the quote: *There is always room for improvement*, automatically identifies that if a person has done their best, that their best was not good enough! Even convincing someone that they need to move out of their comfort zone to gain better results, again, is pressure to strive further.

The messages people receive from employers, teachers, lecturers, personal trainers, etc that they have to push, push harder, and keep on pushing identifies no limits! Yet you need limits to know that you are not exerting yourself physically mentally, emotionally, and spiritually. Like setting boundaries, you also need to set limits if you are to promote self-care and when you feel you have pushed yourself as far as you can go, this is where you need to take time out to rest and recuperate, re-evaluate and re-energise. Although more often than not, people refuse to connect to how they feel and instead focus on their thoughts, which were generated by external demands and other people's agendas. This is where original healthy limits are bypassed, and not even replaced with any other limit, so where originally you had a comfortable, steady, life journey pace, this then morphed from the likes of a passenger train into an express train, and if there are still no limits put in place your life journey can then morph into what feels like a runaway train. This, unfortunately, is where people identify with a feeling of not only lacking in control but out of control.

Setting yourself healthy limits is a must in all areas of life! This is not only for your mental health but also for your emotional health, spiritual and also your physical health. Reflect on all areas of your life, and attempt to identify where you do not have any limits, consider why this is, and maybe even set about creating limits in order to prioritise yourself. Setting a limit is where you say to yourself, 'Enough is enough!' or 'No more!' and where you connect to assertiveness and say to other people, 'No!' or even 'Not now!' Assertiveness is a must when setting limits as this is not only for your own information but for the information of others who may have a tendency to take advantage.

The absence of limits creates pressure, pressure creates stress and unfortunately, stress affects your nervous system, turning on your stress response hormone (Cortisol), and so your body now perceives this as a threat. In turn, your body then turns on your primitive survival instinct of flight, fight, or freeze! So, for as long as you are experiencing this threat to your peace, you are now living on a daily basis, in survival mode. This is a much-heightened state of awareness and says nothing about inadequacies connected to self, but a very natural reaction to a very unnatural situation. You were born to be in control of yourself, and if you are not, your body will be.

Unfortunately, over time your body becomes accustomed to this Cortisol release, from prolonged periods of stressful situations, and therefore when you are not even in a stressful situation, your body will still expect this Cortisol discharge. This is the reason people are unable to relax even when they have an opportunity to because the brain is in an expectant mode.

Too much Cortisol can also reduce our immune system, causing a variety of physical problems, and can produce diseases such as high blood pressure, heart disease, high blood sugar, and digestive issues.

Also, living constantly in this heightened state eventually has a detrimental effect on your mental abilities, i.e., concentrating or focusing on a task. This is the case whether you are actually in a stressful situation, or you are simply thinking (worrying) about a stressful situation, so it is now your thoughts that are making you ill, and unfortunately, you can even become addicted to your own thoughts!

Therefore, to begin taking back control from your body and your thoughts, and so bringing about healing, it is not you who needs to change, but your situation!

When you begin to take back control by quitting that job, ending that unhealthy relationship, or even having an adult conversation with your parents with regard to this being your life, you begin to reduce this stress, and so move from living in survival to living in creation. This is where you can connect to faith in your own capabilities of being master of your own life and destiny.

Changes will not happen overnight as healing is not light flicking a switch, it begins with baby steps, but the aim is not to get frustrated with yourself and expect that some days will be better than others. You will have to force yourself to relax, which does not necessarily mean doing nothing, this can include reading a book or magazine, going for a walk alone, or with your dog if you have one (or someone else's dog even!). You could even lie down and simply listen to music, but whatever you decide to do, commit yourself to do this for at least ten minutes initially, increasing this by five more minutes each time you participate in some form of relaxation. Yes, you will feel agitated, and it will be so easy to say, 'I can't do this.' But the focus has to be on healing, and so dedication, commitment, and persistence are what is needed here to bring about this healing. You owe this to yourself; you are worthy of a happy and healthy life.

Section Three
Emotional

Okay, so let us now talk about emotions because it is okay to talk about emotions! Regardless of what you have been told, or advised, up until this point! To laugh with joy, squeal with delight, cry with sadness, scream and shout in anger, or howl like a banshee with devastation, this is all okay to do too!

And let us also identify that people who presently struggle with their health and their emotions as a result of experiencing either a traumatic childhood, a traumatic relationship, having engaged in a traumatic career (forces, police, fire service or ambulance service, to name a few) or even having experienced one singular traumatic incident, are not damaged! They are simply wounded.

As we can suffer from a physical injury so too can we suffer from an emotional injury! Just because this type of injury cannot be seen with the naked eye does not mean this type of injury does not exist.

So, first and foremost, it is for people to cease labelling themselves as 'damaged' (as a result of an external locus of evaluation) and acknowledge themselves as simply someone in need of healing for their emotional wounds.

This is about having their brain take a back seat and allowing them to connect with their emotions. Acknowledging that this pain and suffering exists, as opposed to being in denial or attempting to run away from it, each time this wound gets poked, and so the emotions get triggered.

In the animal kingdom, a wounded animal does not simply embrace an attempt from someone to assist; it will first and foremost go on the attack. This is by way of protecting themselves from being hurt further. Similarly, humans initially resist help and support, because in acknowledging their wound to someone else, they also have to acknowledge this wound to themselves. They feel that if someone saw the extent of the damage, they would not be able to deal with it, and so having exposed this vulnerability and it not having been cured, this will then feel like they have been rejected. So, rather than suffer this rejection (especially if this has happened to them previously when they have asked for help) they choose to live in denial. Although, even if people feel they cannot expose this wound to others, they are not alone in their discomfort, as unconditional love and support are closer than they think, and they can choose to connect to a higher energy for help through meditation.

You are your greatest ally, and until you heal this wound, the wounded part in you will seek out the wounded part in others, as emotionally wounded people who feel unable to heal themselves, will attempt to heal the wounded part in others, as compensation. This is why people bounce from bad relationship to bad relationship as it does not have a healthy foundation to begin with, and even though wounded people have this need to heal others, the other may not even want to be healed! So straight away we have conflict.

Reflect on your relationships to date, do you feel they were healthy? What do you consider your role was in that relationship? Did you see yourself as a rescuer at all? Or you may have even seen yourself in the role of a nurturing parent?

If you are hiding a wound from people, then you are also concealing your authentic self, and being unable to be who you truly are (as a result of this wound or wounds) you will simply be playing a role.

Eric Berne, a Canadian-born psychiatrist, created the theory of transactional analysis, in which he identified that in taking on a role, we are simply playing games. That could be relationship games, power games with bosses, or competitive games with our friends. He put his findings in a book, which he entitled, *The games people play*, in which he reveals manoeuvres that rule our lives unconsciously. Although, through self-reflection, you can put an end to any games that you play.

A student of Dr Bern's, a man called Stephen Karpman, used triangles to map out conflict in drama, intense relationship games or interactions. *The Karpman Drama Triangle,* portrays the connection between personal responsibility and power in conflicts and the destructive and shifting roles people play. He identified three possible roles in a particular conflict, namely 'Persecutor', 'Rescuer' and 'Victim'. Karpman placed these three roles in an inverted triangle and referred to them as being the three aspects or faces of drama. And, subconsciously, at any given time throughout the day, people can shift between roles depending on different interactions that they are involved in, and with whom.

The persecutor is seen as the villain of the drama triangle, always pointing the finger to lay blame at another's feet. They see themselves as superior and authoritarian, they are rigid, controlling, oppressive, blaming, and critical. Never taking ownership or responsibility for anything and simply embracing the motto of, *I am in charge.*

The rescuer feels guilty if they do not go to the rescue, their motto being; *Let me help you*, yet their rescuing has negative effects, as it keeps the victim dependent on them. Benefits for being in the rescue role are that focus is taken off them, as this role enables them to ignore their own anxiety and issues. This rescuer role is a role of avoidance disguised as concern for the victim's needs.

The victim is not an actual victim, but simply someone feeling or acting like one. Their motto is; *Poor me*, the victim feels helpless, hopeless, and powerless, and appears unable to make decisions, solve problems, or take pleasure in life. The Victim, if not being persecuted, will actually seek out a persecutor as well as a rescuer, who of course will save the day, and also clarify the victim's present negative feelings about themselves.

In another area of transactional analysis which Dr Berne developed, he identified that people can also switch between different states of mind in the same conversation, and also in different areas of their lives, such as at work or at home. He proposed that these states of mind combined became three different types, which he named as 'Parent', 'Adult' and 'Child'.

The 'Child' identity consists of parts of ourselves, which connect us to our childhood, although it is childlike, not childish. In this identity, we are connected to our intuition and creativity, we have impulsive behaviour and are fun-seeking.

The 'Parent' identity reflects taking on ownership over the years of the influences of their own parents and taking on the responsibility of a parent and other authority figures such as teachers and bosses. This role, therefore, has two responsibilities. Firstly, to enable people to be better parents of their own children, and the other is to take responsibility and to make decisions with authority.

The 'Adult' identity is what people hope to be as adults. It is our adult selves, dealing with the unpleasantries of everyday life. It also has the function of regulating the activities of the 'Parent' and 'Child' and attempting to resolve any conflict between them.

Those in the role of 'child' can also be compared to that of the victim; similarly, those in the role of persecutor can be seen as having the parent persona. Although this is made even more apparent by identifying a specific angle of this theory, 'authoritative parent'. In addition, 'nurturing parent' is a second angle.

The child role does not simply portray childlike behaviour as immaturity and lacking responsibility, but also, conformity in this role as 'adaptive child' or rebellion as an 'angry child'.

People, unfortunately, confuse their responses with an adult who is simply responding to the situation, when in fact they are playing out one of the above roles.

To interact in a healthy way would be to identify if you are in a drama triangle and to make the decision to remove yourself, also to identify that you are in fact an adult, capable of making your own choices and decisions. A definition of adult is someone who takes ownership and responsibility for their own life, someone who has an awareness of never having to explain or justify themselves to anyone, (about anything) and having an acceptance that they will make mistakes, but also that they will learn from these mistakes and evolve mentally, emotionally, and spiritually as a result.

Therefore, in order to be who you were truly meant to be, and interact with others as your core self, it would be beneficial to be mindful of portraying any of these roles, and also of playing any games, by bringing this from the subconscious to the conscious. You will not know unless you self-reflect, and here, you can begin a transformation. To be who we were truly meant to be is emotional freedom.

Bear in mind the above are only roles that are played out as a result of lack of awareness; they are not labels, although diagnostic labels can, unfortunately, be assigned wherever and whenever it is deemed appropriate. Adults who were labelled with a diagnosis connected to their behaviour as children could feel stuck with this diagnosis (or label) for life, even when medication ended years before! This could possibly be the root of emotional anguish.

Although some labels are debatable from a spiritual perspective! The New Age Journal says that most, *Indigo children*, have been wrongly diagnosed with ADD / ADHD and are acting out to usher in a new way of doing things, in respect of human evolution. The indigo children phenomenon began in the 1970s by psychic Nancy Ann Tappe, who published a book about this concept called, *Understanding Your Life through Colour*. Nancy noticed that a large number of children were being born with indigo auras, (an aura is just a field of energy surrounding our physical form, which can change colour depending on mood and the environment:

which can be seen through practice). Nancy ascertained that these 'indigo children' represented the next stage in human evolution and possessed traits of being more creative and more empathetic than their peers and also have less patience with mundane or uninteresting learning.

So, research this phenomenon more if you choose to, and identify if the description given of an 'indigo child' resonates with you?

Crystal children, is another description given for children born more recently than in the 1970s.

To feel different can cause extreme emotional anguish as a child especially during school years, as children do not generally want to feel set apart from their peers. This cannot only be connected to feeling less than their peers due to an unhealthy childhood but also from being made to feeling superior. This is known as, *Emperor Syndrome*.

Child psychologist Dr Amanda Gummer agrees that parents naturally want to give their children everything they need, although she says that some parents can give their children much more attention than is really needed. Excessive amounts of attention from parents and grandparents can cause children to have suicidal thoughts, and so they become an increased suicide risk if they feel that there are no boundaries. Children need rules, boundaries, and opportunities to feel the cold, go hungry and fall down and hurt themselves, so they can learn from their mistakes, and if they are deprived of those basic life experiences at home, it makes becoming educated or in later life employed, more difficult for them.

Excessive attention can cause a child to connect with a feeling of entitlement and this may not go down well with their classmates! So, what happens then is that they become alienated from them, with no inclination as to what they have done wrong. They are simply behaving how they have been taught to, by their needs and wants always being prioritised and without having been taught to share, do things for themselves, or face appropriate consequences for unacceptable behaviour. Children can then face an existence of confusion and frustration, resulting in depression in adult life, or even in childhood.

To have endured an unhealthy childhood makes for someone who experiences emotional anguish or depression understandable, although thinking that you had a privileged childhood could prevent you from identifying a possible reason for experiencing depression.

As mentioned earlier on in this book, we are capable of producing our own serotonin and dopamine, connected to participating in pleasant activities and interests. Although as a child, the discovery of a new activity, or gaining pride or pleasure from accomplishing a task also has this effect. But, if a child has never been given the opportunity to discover this potential, due to parents constantly providing their entertainment, or even completing their school homework for them, they, unfortunately, learn not to look! And simply wait to be provided.

In adulthood, friends, neighbours, colleagues, and partners expect you to know how to provide for yourself, whether that be provisions, domestics, or pass times. But having never been taught how to, as an adult you will struggle with these simple tasks, and with the expectations of others. More so, however, this struggle could result also in depression. Frustration and confusion can prevent someone from seeing clearly, although this frustration is connected to a lack of knowledge and understanding.

Self-reflection is extremely valuable in identifying possible causes for depression, and not simply just by thinking, but by writing in a journal what you remember from your childhood. Through this self-reflection and journaling, you will gain epiphanies (light bulb moments) of realisation and understanding, and so you will become less frustrated with not only your life in general but less frustrated (and angry) with yourself!

This is not to say journaling will be a miracle cure for depression, healing is dependent on how long someone has experienced this, and how much effort they put into their healing journey. This condition (and I call it condition and not illness deliberately) can be resolved in time, and the amount of time that is needed cannot be predetermined. Overcoming depression, like grief, will take as long as is needed and if not, enough time is dedicated to this, then of course results will not be forthcoming.

In an ideal world, taking time away from work until you feel one hundred percent healthy would be phenomenal, although having commitments and bills to pay prevents this, meaning that a condensed course of healing is unimaginable. Juggling work and commitments, and also completing a healing journey, will, of course, take longer to obtain the desired results, but focusing on the journey and not the desired outcome, will have an even more profound effect.

To live in avoidance or denial, and suppressing your emotional anguish through embarrassment, lack of time, other commitments etc, will ultimately result in depression, or suicidal thoughts. But, through exploration, the cause of the depression (possible confusion and frustration) can be discovered, and the connection to the frustration and confusion can also be uncovered. Acknowledgement, understanding and even acceptance allow eventually for depression to be replaced with inner peace.

Even when acknowledging the negative messages and mistaken beliefs that have originated externally, it is also worth recognising that your own clarification of these is what is keeping you where you are. As the saying goes, 'If you always do what you have always done, you will always get what you have always got', so even if at present you are convinced and you believe these unhealthy thoughts about yourself, it is you who is keeping these beliefs alive, and to entertain the idea of telling yourself the opposite, will, of course, feel ridiculous to you. But this is what you must do in order to bring about change, repeating phrases, reciting mantras, reading positive affirmations, daily, all go toward bringing about the structural changes in your brain, and depending on how often you do these things depends on how quickly you will begin to see a change taking place. Although you cannot stop there, because that is just notification to yourself that a new neural connection has been established, the next aim, of course, is to strengthen, lengthen and thicken this new neural pathway until these healthier thoughts and beliefs become automatic pilot. Taking ownership and responsibility is paramount on a healing journey, a therapist can provide the tools to restore your brain garden, but it is you who does all the work. Even if it feels like a pointless task, do it anyway, even if it feels like you are getting nowhere, do it anyway, in fact, it is said that we can create a new habit after doing it for twenty-one days, although others say twenty-one times (irrespective of how many days), I say, recite the mantra's twenty-one times over twenty-one days! Because of course repetition is the key here!

Marisa Peer (2018) identifies, *I am enough,* as an excellent quote for bringing about change in self-esteem and self-worth, she connects this belief to all areas of our being reciting that, we are intelligent enough, beautiful enough, clever enough, capable enough, etc and also encourages her clients to memorise this quote:

I am enough.
I have always been enough.
Now that I know | I am enough.
I will always be enough.

Try reciting this twenty-one times for twenty-one days, whilst looking at yourself in a mirror, but look deep into your eyes and tell this to your spirit.

People are their own worst critics, yet you ought to be singing your own praises!

The very fact that you are struggling confirms what a sensitive person you are, and people, unfortunately, attack what they do not understand, so simply because someone criticises does not make it fact! It only confirms that they do not understand your sensitivity, hopefully, one day they will, but even if they never do that is okay, as long as you cease absorbing this criticism.

Whatever hurt you have had to endure, there is always a way back from the deepest, darkest, and dankest pit that someone can find themselves in, even if that means having someone walk in there to greet you (spiritually) take your hand whilst you tell your story, and then guide you back into the light of life. This can take place with a trustworthy friend (or a therapist), anyone who is prepared to go on this journey with you, provided they confirm your emotional state is healthy prior to leaving you, and that you have support close by afterwards. You may have heard the quote: *It is good to talk,* and it is! Releasing suppressed emotions is physically, mentally, emotionally, and spiritually healing.

Although, if you feel unable to speak to someone, then tell your story on paper, write it down and let it out. Even if this is connected to grief, and you possibly never had the opportunity to say goodbye to a loved one, then write a 'goodbye letter' to the one you are missing, this too has a similar healing effect. This letter could then be kept behind their photograph in a frame, or even taken to a special place and buried in the ground, whatever feels better for yourself to do, but know that you are acknowledging this, and not simply 'getting on with it' or 'moving on' as is the pressure for everyone to do by society. This parting would not only be connected to people but also animals, as the love people feel for their pets is just as strong and natural, irrespective of other people's opinion, this is about you, not them!

Anyone who has experienced hurt in childhood, which has been directed deliberately by primary caregivers, leads to feelings of frustration. This is due to the child not being able to escape this unhealthy treatment, and so eventually frustration deepens into anger. Furthermore, feeling powerless in this situation, the anger simply gets suppressed, until unfortunately it is triggered, usually when in a relationship as an adult.

Domestic violence manifests from these triggers (reminders) of feeling powerless and helpless, and this could simply be one word or an expression that a perpetrator would use.

So now some of that suppressed anger is released but directed toward the wrong person.

Acknowledging to yourself that you experienced an unhealthy childhood and releasing this anger by way of either writing a 'no send' letter or participating in the 'empty chair' exercise does really come with benefits! No, you are not dealing directly with the perpetrator and you don't need to! They do not need to be present for you to cuss and curse at them, but the results are the same! Release and relief! If you or anyone you know has pent up anger toward any aggressor for any reason, give either of these exercises a try, they do help.

To explain, the 'empty chair' technique is a talking therapy exercise in which you express your thoughts and feelings as if you were talking to a specific person. Even though that person is not present, you direct your words and gestures at an empty chair and imagine that person sitting facing toward you while you talk.

The person you need to talk to could be emotionally unavailable or deceased, but it can still help to express your anger as if they were sitting there in front of you. You simply set up a chair across from you and pretend that the person you need to talk to is sitting in it, then say or shout whatever you want to, to that person.

Just say whatever comes to your mind, but if you find it difficult to get started, and if you struggle to imagine that the person is sitting there, don't worry about it. Just start saying whatever comes to your mind when you begin thinking of this person, and as you begin talking, you will feel as if you're talking directly to that person.

Releasing suppressed anger in a safe way and in a safe environment is far healthier for everyone connected to a domestic violence situation and also prevents suppressed anger from being triggered on an evening out.

Emotional Freedom Technique (EFT) is another form of therapy that can also help to release suppressed anger, and this therapy can be performed on yourself by yourself.

EFT was developed by Gary Craig in the 1990s, although this is a simplified version of Thought Field Therapy (TFT), which was developed by Roger Callahan in the 1980s. This therapy focuses on unblocking meridians, which are energy points throughout the body and are explained further in the next section. Callahan focussed his therapy on three hundred and sixty-five meridians, although Craig reduced this number to only eleven, being at specific parts of the body.

This therapy consists of simply bringing together your index finger and middle finger, and whilst you are focussing on a specific phobia or an issue that causes you anxiety (and also identifying this fear is at a level often) you then tap on a specific meridian point with these fingers, whilst reducing the numbers, down through 9, 8, 7, etc, until you arrive at zero. The aim therefore is whilst you are reducing the numbers, you are also reducing your anxiety, and as this has produced spectacular results, do not knock it until you try it!

Although of course feeling unhealthy emotionally is not simply about feeling anxious, experiencing depression is more of a struggle, with people experiencing one or the other or both at the same time. Often people can know the word depression but not understand its meaning or symptoms, and whereas anxiety can cause a Person to feel hyper or agitated, depression manifests in the opposite way, by causing the sufferer to feel lethargic with no energy or interest in anything.

Depression can be described as deep sadness and can manifest for many reasons including: having experienced disloyalty, betrayal, or simply things or people in your life turning out differently than you expected. One huge mistake people make is expecting people to be all the same, but of course, they are not! However, you see yourself, yes you will meet people who will think and act like you, but you will also meet people who do not, and so it is our expectations that really disappoint us, not people! But having said that, it is the disappointment, which people find themselves having to deal with. Depending on how much you feel this disappointment, will then reflect in the depth of your sadness.

So let us now identify some expectations, that could lead to disappointment: expecting parents or siblings to be loyal and supportive simply because they are family, is a huge expectation, yet they are people just like you, with their own wants, needs and agendas and who are possibly prioritising themselves which as mentioned previously, is a good thing. Although if you expect people to drop everything when you need them to, and they do not, you could see this as them being unsupportive, although where did that expectation of yours come from? And are you right about this expectation?

By the same token if you have made a mutual promise or commitment with someone to be of mutual support, and, you have supported them previously, but when there comes a time that you need their support and they are unwilling to dedicate any of their time and effort to you, then yes you could not be blamed for feeling let down or betrayed.

Also, to have been involved with an unfaithful partner could further lead to feelings of betrayal, especially if you have always considered yourself faithful and loyal toward them.

Although, whatever the circumstances, your emotions are real, your pain and your hurt. Especially if you feel betrayal has happened to you more than once, and your expectations of those you depended on were based on what you have invested in this commitment.

You could also feel let down or betrayed by someone passing away because you were not ready for him/her to leave you.

Betrayal can feel devastating like you have lost everything, your faith and trust in relationships, and even life in general. Also, the hurt and pain you experience could make you feel debilitated and incapable of performing the simplest tasks, like tidying up, showering, or even conversing with others. Someone experiencing these symptoms could simply appear lazy to observers and in the absence of receiving any concern or support, this could then, unfortunately, exacerbate their situation.

But this is depression, losing sight in a future and in oneself, and the longer a person sits in this place the more familiar it will become, and so anything else presents a threat because it is unknown, as everything that was known, understood, and accepted previously to them, is now alien, because what they considered or expected to be right, turned out to be wrong.

And not to make light of depression but if you collected all the ingredients together to make a pie and once you had put in all that effort and produced a beautiful pie but then it got dropped on the floor that would of course be so disappointing, but guess what? You can make another pie! And in the same respect, you can build another future, you could even choose different ingredients this time, and this time you may even decide you do not want to follow a recipe, and throw all expectations to the side, this time you could decide to be more creative and choose all your own ingredients and measurements because this is your pie! And you have the right to make these choices and decisions. You could choose to share this pie or not like you could decide to share your future or not, but either way, whether someone likes your pie or not, whether someone gives a compliment or not, that does not matter! Because it is just their opinion! If you like your pie that is all that matters! You can decide that no longer will another person's opinion or attitude have any effect on how much you enjoy the taste of your own pie, which you created for yourself.

To use yet another metaphor, imagine a new-born as a new balloon, and this balloon has been inflated by others using toxic gases, then over time the toxic gases have a negative effect on the balloon and it becomes deflated as a result, (the same as our spirit) but, you can then re-inflate this balloon again, using the freshest of air.

When everything you have ever known seems lost to you, when you yourself feel lost, there is always a way forward out of the deep, dark abyss that you find yourself in. An unknown future seems frightening and yet this unknown future that is waiting for you will be better, healthier, and more in tune with your spirit. This does as said previously, involve a journey, and through this journey, you will revisit painful memories, although by doing this you will be reprocessing all the stored information that you have absorbed throughout your entire life so far.

Firstly, you have to acknowledge the pain that you are experiencing, no longer can you deny that you were possibly betrayed and/or abandoned by those who you loved the most, and this acknowledgement will be a very painful pill to swallow. Connect with these emotions, and express the feelings of unhappiness and sadness, once you have ceased suppressing these emotions, and accepted that you are hurting (this also includes breaking through the anger that you have possibly relied on for many years, as your strength, to get you through the day – in order to reach and connect with the root emotion of sadness). This is the first step on your journey, and so moving onto the second step we look into how to heal this sadness but if you choose not to speak to someone then writing is a brilliant way of bringing about this healing, it does not have to involve journaling, or writing an essay, or even writing poetry! Simply let a pen run free on paper and allow whatever surfaces to escape and be freed.

It is better to use pen and paper as the energy frequency of a smartphone or laptop will interfere with your own natural energy frequency. Do not focus on neatness, spelling, or punctuality, this is for you alone and you are not going to be judged, you could even include profanities if you decide to! This is all about you, no one else just let rip! Let yourself go! This is for you to acknowledge the mistreatment you have endured, this is for you to say, 'Hey, this is me, and this is what happened to me!' It does not matter that no one will ever read these words, the healing is in the acknowledgement and giving yourself this attention and recognition.

Acceptance of self is the next step, warts and all! Even with your painful experiences, you are still very much worthy of self-love. Saying, 'This is me, take me or leave me, and my existence does not depend on anyone else's approval or acceptance.'

The final step is self-forgiveness, forgiving yourself for anytime that you feel you have self-criticised or self-sabotaged, whether that be emotionally or physically, you are worthy of forgiveness and you are worthy of self-love. Anything not in line with these beliefs is incorrect, it is your own choice to connect with this self-belief, and you can choose to believe this fact. You will struggle initially, and the old thought patterns will attempt to ridicule you, and try to put you off making changes, but remain persistent, dedicated, committed and eventually, you will succeed.

If you had a broken leg, you would acknowledge this and allow yourself time to heal, well the same applies to a broken spirit and if you feel that you have been knocked down and before you have even had a chance to get back up again, you have been knocked a second time, and possibly this has been repeated and repeated until you feel you have no more energy left to fight, well guess what? You do! It is in the deepest region of your being and it is called love! You are simply energy and energy is love, and even though you have not been able to connect with this until now, you can break down the barriers that are concealing that love and allow it to engulf you, bask in this energy of pure love, this unconditional, pure love energy, it is there, and it is yours for the taking.

Visualise a soft warm cosy, comfortable blanket made from this love, and wrap it around your shoulders, allow this love to soak into the very essence of you, you are entitled to this, and whenever you need a self-love boost, wrap your love blanket around you again and again until you are filled to the brim with self-love.

Even though you may have never had trust in yourself, you can build this trust up, tell yourself in your writing that you will never again, let yourself down, betray yourself, or hurt yourself, build up that trust in yourself and become your own best friend. It could be the child in you that does not trust the adult you, well, reassure your inner child, and nurture him/her by recognising that your inner child is also being wrapped in this blanket of pure love.

The only thing that heals hurt and pain and betrayal is love, and that is not reliant on anyone else, that is only reliant on you, it does not matter that you did not receive the love from parents, or primary caregivers, or siblings or partners that you were expecting because you are so very capable and so very worthy of giving love to yourself! Love from the eternal after this is a bonus, a top-up, but going forward you will still be able to function should they choose to move on, or you make this choice because you are not leaving love behind, you are taking your self-love with you, wherever you go, and it is abundant! It never runs out! You will be able to walk away in health and harmony because you have enough self for this, and it only takes you tapping into this during silence, meditation, or mindfulness, simply by choosing to connect to this love energy.

These steps will take as long as they take, you may write one page or a novel even, which you keep returning to, but there is no time limit on healing as there is no time limit on grieving. The point is, say all that you have to say, and only you know when you have said it all, but with each visit to this exercise, recognise that healing is taking place.

Joseph Campbell identifies a healing journey as a path we take to find our true self (in his book, *The Hero's Journey*), and further, *Finding Joe*, is a programme focussed on his book which amplifies his message.

Initially, you have to be certain that you are following your own path, and not being directed or led by anyone else, also be sure not to follow an already walked path as your path is unique to you! Your own thoughts, visions, and light bulb moments. You can take advantage of what you are experiencing at present and use it as a doorway to an 'awakening', experiencing trauma presents this opportunity although even if someone has never experienced a trauma they can still choose to go on a journey of self-discovery. Whatever you learn or however you change, this is all down to you, no credit should be given to an abuser or perpetrator! You do not become who you are after you complete your journey because of them; you become who you are in spite of them! So, no credit belongs to anyone other than yourself!

Choosing to go on this journey will take you from victim of your own life to hero of your own life, choose to challenge the monsters in your head, face your demons, slay your dragons and in doing so this hero's journey will make you feel alive, rather than simply feeling like you are just existing. What you discover and what you learn on this journey is then your gift to pass on to others, to empower them through your survival, and as a thriver, you then have greater emotional health which you can share. In fact, we are always learning, always growing, and always evolving so the stronger you become the more journeys you can choose to go on, and each time you will attain even more knowledge and insight, and so become even stronger!

You are then able to write or tell your story of growth to inspire and empower others; this is what life is all about: you are the pupil and the teacher at the same time! You learn and you share and as in learning you evolve, so too do you evolve in sharing, and the way you will feel emotionally in sharing is spiritually rewarding.

Fear is the thing that prevents people from choosing to do this, although you are not moving out of your comfort zone at all, you will simply be increasing the size of it. You were not born with fear, you learned it and so too can you unlearn it! Explore your fear, where did it come from? Who put it there? Not you! Your inner strength is far greater than your fear, you have just never been able to discover it, or connect with it. Fear is not a fact, it is simply an emotion created by a thought, yet you have the power to change those thoughts. A drug of choice allows that fear to be masked (prescribed or nonprescribed), alcohol, shopping, work, or gambling they all subdue the frustration and so prevents self-discovery.

You have huge potential; you have just never been able to identify or acknowledge that until now, and you have an inherent passion to grow and evolve, and it has only been through others' agendas that you have not been able to. But you can move beyond the confines of fear, you can reclaim your own power, which is deep within you, and has always been there, of course, if you have never searched to connect you will not know it is there, but it is, it is in all of us. You were not born to struggle; you were not born to be a victim, you can move past and move beyond suffering, and connecting to this possibility of change is the first step.

As emotions run deep so does healing happen at the deepest level, in fact, we could liken these depths to the ground beneath our feet. Initially, on first inspection, we are presented with what is called the organic layer, which is a thick film of dead leaves and twigs for all to see, this could be identified as the public persona that you present to the world, what you allow strangers to see.

Directly beneath this organic layer is the topsoil, which is a fairly thin layer only five to ten inches thick, composed of organic matter and minerals. This layer is the primary layer where plants and organisms live. And so, this would be the initial element of you, that you possibly allow being seen by your neighbours and work colleagues.

Subsoil comes next and is made primarily of clay, iron, and organic matter which accumulated through a process called illuviation. This is a little more of you that you show to people who you consider friends.

Next is the parent material layer, which is called the parent material because the upper layers developed from this layer and is made up mostly of large rocks. This is the part of you that you chose to hide as a result of hurtful experiences, and therefore this is the part of your personality that is covered and so protected, which no one gets to see.

The bottom layer is several feet below the surface and is called bedrock, this is made up of a large solid mass of rock, and this is where your 'authentic self' hidden, covered by denial and avoidance mechanisms.

A therapeutic journey is a journey of discovery, excavation and exploration down through the layers. To venture on this journey takes courage and trust and is sometimes best taken with a stranger (therapist) so at the end of this journey, you can emerge as the you that you were meant to be, who you can then show to everyone you ever come into contact with.

No one else ever needs to know any of this information unless you choose to disclose it. You could decide that once this, deep and possibly historic part of you has been acknowledged it can all be left in the counselling room where it was excavated and walk away from there as the real you, absent of all and anything that has ever held you back from embracing your authentic self.

Another comparison would be:

On the surface, your question could possibly be: 'What would change'? During therapeutic exploration, deriving from the physical (logical thinking brain).

The next deeper level could be your concern of: 'How could things change?' Coming from your mental capacity, wanting information.

An even deeper level would derive from emotional concern 'How would I bring about this change and how would this affect me?'

Then, ultimately on the spiritual level, this would be about embracing inner strength, wanting to bring about this change.

Change is all about overcoming your fears, embracing courage, and connecting with your inner strength, which you have an abundance of, but you have not been allowed to acknowledge up until this point.

Decide to not continue living a lie, if it feels wrong that is because it is! If you are not satisfied with your life, change it! Change your job, sell your house, and move area or to somewhere bigger or smaller, whatever you feel will suit you. Identify the frustration you feel and choose to get off the treadmill! If you feel you are living a mundane life, connect with your passion and work toward what you want and how you want your life to look like. Everything requires a transitional period though, things do not change in the flick of a button, imagine where you are now is a block circle and where you want to be is a white circle, visualise this and bring them close together until they overlap, the centre part now becomes a grey colour, and this is a step on the journey to living the life you want. But you have to pass through this slightly difficult transitional stage to reach the white area.

'Seek and you will find'! Stop self-sabotaging your possible future by remaining in your (unhealthy) comfort zone, follow your dreams, your inner strength will allow you to connect to the real you, push through the resistance like a snake shedding its skin, the caterpillar spending time in a chrysalis to emerge as a butterfly, the phoenix re-emerging from the flames, reborn, so too can you go through a transitional stage. Think of this as the death of the old you and the re-birth of the new authentic you. Living your own life, you connect to a willingness to rid yourself of the stifled version of yourself and embrace the possibility of change. This new life is waiting for you, contentment, serenity, and inner peace!

Up to now you have neglected and betrayed your spirit, by constantly being embroiled in a battle with your brain (your learned behaviour) and this has caused you to be in debt to your spirit, well now it is time to end this inner battle, prioritise yourself, and so pay off this debt to your spirit.

Connecting to self-forgiveness, self-acceptance, and self-love is your birth right! You only think you are not entitled because this is what you have been taught, but guess what? You are capable and can teach yourself differently.

Begin by accepting your flaws! We all have them, but so what? You are not and never were meant to be perfect, your imperfections make you who you are, your authentic self! And if some cannot accept these flaws then detach from these relationships! You are perfect just as you are!

Now try this exercise: close your eyes and reach out to embrace the non-conditional accepting love energy that completely surrounds you, imagine it to be like huge white fluffy clouds, reach out and grab two armfuls then pull it towards you until you feel engulfed, now allow it to be absorbed by you, and then connect to that feeling of warmth and comfort. Sit for a short while in that space of pure love, and allow yourself to feel fulfilled, do this as often as you feel the need to, love is simply energy, and we are surrounded by it.

Sometimes feeling despondent can have nothing whatsoever to do with being involved in a traumatic event or being brought up in a volatile family setting, it can simply be connected to a feeling that there is something missing in your life (not connected to being without a relationship or not having children). This emotion can be a result of you thinking that you have no reason or purpose in your life, although this is because you have simply not connected to that reason and purpose yet.

Everyone has his own specific vocation or mission in life to carry out a concrete assignment, which demands fulfilment.

Therein, he cannot be replaced, nor can his life be repeated. Thus, everyone's task is as unique as his specific opportunity to implement it. (Frankl, 2004, p. 113).

When you choose to disconnect from everyone else's opinions of what career path you should take, or how you should live your life, and so let your true self shine through (your own passions and your own desires) only then will you be able to begin a journey of rebirth. The courage and inner strength have always been there within you, to connect to and implement assertiveness and so take control over your own life.

If someone has never been assertive, they could, unfortunately, confuse this with aggression and confrontation, although liken assertiveness to kicking a ball around a football pitch, your aim is to put the ball into the goalmouth, but if you kick the ball with too much force it will shoot upward and over the top! And so not provide the result you wanted. Therefore, in order not to shoot beyond your expectations and possibly border onto aggression and confrontation, you simply need to create an awareness of the pitch and tone of your voice! Implement mindfulness at this point, focus on yourself initially, and on remaining calm, also connect attention to how you want to communicate with this other person.

Ultimately, you want to remain in control, control over yourself is empowerment, by not allowing this interaction to steal inner peace from you. State your case as calmly and as precisely as you possibly can, but always be aware of your boundaries possibly being challenged, although, in this instance, you would again connect to mindfulness, in recognising that you do not choose to become embroiled in a heated discussion, and so you would resist any attempt by other people to instigate this, and so you will remain in control of your emotions.

It is your birth right to state your own case, and you are entitled to prioritise yourself, so own and absorb this truth!

By stating your choices, you are taking back control, which you possibly feel you do not have at present. This is your life and the definition of being an adult is taking ownership and responsibility, and provided you are over eighteen years of age and you do not harm others, you are entitled to take ownership and responsibility of your own life.

Taking control of your life is also about taking control of your emotions, and this does not mean suppressing them! In suppressing emotions, you are using avoidance and defence mechanisms, although to allow those emotions to surface at your pace and on your terms, this would be you being in control.

Imagine a bottle of fizzy drink that has been shaken up, this is similar to suppressed anger and frustration, bubbling below the surface, and so if someone were to open that bottle at this point, of course, the contents will surge upwards and spill out uncontrollably. Now liken this to a trigger causing suppressed anger in someone to be released uncontrolled. Therefore, to control the contents of that fizzy drink bottle, you would release the bottle top very slowly, allowing only a small portion of the pressure to be released. You would then continue to slowly open up the bottle top to release even more of the pressure inside until you feel all of the pressure has been released, and so the contents are now calm and controlled and the top can be taken off completely.

This is the same with us, humans, you have to release this suppressed anger and frustration to enjoy a better quality of life, but slowly, at your pace, and in your own time, and like the fizzy drink bottle, eventually all of this unpleasant pressure will have been released, and what remains will be only calmness. No longer will you be able to be triggered, because there will be no unpleasant emotions there to trigger.

As humans, we are capable of an array of emotions although so far, I have only mentioned a few i.e., anger, sadness and happiness yet included in our emotional catalogue we can also include anticipation, fear, loneliness, jealousy, disgust, surprise, and trust. Each of these emotions are to be recognised and embraced in order to gain complete control over them all, and so to be able to do this you have to create emotional awareness.

Emotional awareness is having the ability to understand your own emotions and the effect they have on how you interact with others. In order for you to be able to do this, we can explore an explanation or definition of each, and in addition, I have also included a poem to express each of these emotions. I shall list them in the order outlined above with the exception of one, as I chose 'happiness' to be the final emotion to close this list with.

Anger: this is an emotion characterised by antagonism toward someone or something you feel has deliberately done you wrong. It can actually be a good thing, as it can give you a way to express negative feelings, for example, or motivate you to find solutions to problems. Although excessive anger can cause problems such as increased blood pressure. Although other physical changes associated with anger can make it difficult for you to think straight and possibly harm your physical and mental health (Kazdin, 2000).

There are actually three types of anger, which identify how we react in a situation that makes us angry. They are: Passive Aggression, Open Aggression, and Assertive Anger.

Passive-aggressive behaviour is actioned by any negative thoughts or feelings towards a person or situation, being delivered through actions (instead of these being dealt with verbally). This then creates separation between what someone says and what they actually do!

For instance, say someone puts forward a plan at work. A person with passive-aggressive behaviour may oppose the plan, but instead of voicing their opinion, they agree with it verbally. Although, since they are actually against the plan, they do not follow it! They may deliberately miss deadlines, turn up late to meetings, or undermine this plan in other ways.

Another example is: A person is together with someone else in the same room studying but is upset with this other person, and instead of verbalising that they are upset, they choose to blast out music in order to disturb them.

Other signs of passive-aggressive behaviour are:

Bitterness and hostility toward other peoples' requests.

Intentionally delaying or making mistakes when dealing with other peoples' requests having a cynical, pessimistic, or aggressive demeanour frequently complaining about feeling underappreciated or deceived Passive-aggressive behaviour can be a symptom of some mental health disorders, although it is not considered to be a mental health condition. This type of behaviour can affect a person's ability to create and maintain healthy relationships and can also cause problems at work.

Although, there are ways to manage passive-aggressive behaviour so that it will not have a negative impact on a person's quality of life.

Some signs of passive-aggressive behaviour:

There is usually some disconnect between what a person with passive-aggressive behaviour says and what they do. Their behaviour would anger family members, friends, and colleagues. However, the person displaying these signs are generally unaware that this is passive-aggressive behaviour.

Examples of this behaviour could include:

Frequently criticising or protesting being disagreeable or irritable, procrastinating or being forgetful performing tasks inefficiently, acting hostile or cynical, acting stubborn blaming others complaining about being unappreciated, displaying resentment over the demands of others (Martel, 2021).

Open aggression is the most obvious expression of anger. They are explosive episodes, yelling, name-calling, blaming shifting, and also physical violence. It is self-preservation of needs, and convictions, although it comes at other people's expense. It also does not have to be an explosive rage though, it can also be criticising others, arguing, silent treatment, and sarcasm.

Often, open aggression stems from a deep wound having been mistreated in some way, and you might have learned from past experiences that the only way to get people to listen to you and take you seriously is to shout! Open aggression feels powerful, as it prevents others from hurting you, and so it feels like you are in control, it also often feels like it is the only option open to you. Someone was wronging you, eh? What were you supposed to do? Just sit back and take it?

Your needs are somewhat legitimate, and of course, you are worthy of respect, but open aggression presents itself when you focus on your own personal needs and so completely overshadow the needs of others. This results in huge insensitivity, making you incapable of taking another person's needs into account. Your hurt and your needs are so great that it feels like you have the right to do whatever you can to get what you need and protect yourself (VanRheenen, 2018).

Using assertive anger allows you to resolve conflicts in a way that is productive and respectful to all concerned. It means that you are talking about the situation that has caused disharmony in an attempt to resolve the situation and without hurting other people's feelings.

A person using assertive anger is looking for a win/win solution for everyone concerned. They want to get rid of their anger towards someone and not make it worse. The assertive person has the ability to be kind and respectful of other people's needs as well as with their own.

Assertive anger is calm and respectful. And an assertive person does not need to use aggression, confrontation or cause an argument. They just needed to state how they feel so that the issue or conflict can be resolved.

Traits of Assertive Anger:

Confidence
Self-respect
Respectful of others
Polite
Straightforward and to-the-point
Responsible

Mature
Kind
Stands up for themselves

Assertive Anger includes:
Softer or lower tone of voice
The use of hand gestures
Direct eye contact when talking and listening
Relaxed posture
Talking and asking questions (Deboni, 2021).

When people talk about dealing with their demons, these demons can simply be unresolved anger, so when we resolve the anger, we release the demons!

The following poem is entitled, *Demons!*

There are no more demons in the dark they weren't there any way they were in my head put there by others wanting me not to be myself demons of confusion and pain like wolves with yellow eyes in a black forest lost, cold, alone except for the heat of disapproval from anger and disappointment of others never good enough, never pleasing now, the demons have gone!

No longer do I try to please so no longer the pain or the demons!

You see, you can rid yourself of anything that you consider demons.

Sadness: The universal trigger for sadness is the loss of a valued person or object, although this can vary greatly based on a personal definition of value and loss.

Common sadness triggers are:
Rejection by a friend or lover
Endings and goodbyes
Sickness or death of a loved one

The loss of some aspect of identity (e.g., during times of transition at home, work, life stages)

Being disappointed by an unexpected outcome (e.g., not receiving a raise at work when you expected it)

Moods and disorders.

The key difference between mood and emotion is duration, and how long it lasts. Sadness is a long-lasting emotion and often moves through periods of protest, resignation, and helplessness. It is also important to note that sadness is different from depression, which is of course serious and described as recurrent, persistent, and intense feelings of sadness and hopelessness that interfere with daily living (Ekman, 2021).

Sadness also helps us appreciate happiness. When our mood eventually changes from sadness toward happiness, the sense of contrast adds to the enjoyment of the mood.

Here are some ways in which to experience normal sadness in healthy ways and to allow this emotion to enrich your life:

Allow yourself to be sad! Denying these feelings causes them to be suppressed and then can do more damage with time. Cry whenever you feel like it, and notice that you feel relief after the tears stop.

Write in a journal, listen to music, spend time with friends or family, even think about drawing to possibly express this sadness.

Think about what brought on the sad feelings. Are they related to a loss or an unhappy event? Don't judge yourself and simply ride the wave of this experience.

Sadness can result from a change that you didn't expect, or it can even signal that you might need to make changes in your life. Emotions are forever changing, and this will eventually pass. Although, we should become aware when sadness turns into depression and get help if this happens rather than ignoring and suppressing this.

Signs of Depression are:

Depressed mood (e.g., feeling sad or empty)

Lack of interest in previously enjoyable activities

Significant weight loss or gain, a decrease or increase in appetite

Insomnia or hypersomnia

Agitation, restlessness, irritability

Fatigue or loss of energy

Feelings of worthlessness, hopelessness, and guilt

Inability to think or concentrate, or indecisiveness

Recurrent thoughts of death, recurrent suicidal ideation, suicide attempt or plan (Gundersen, 2021).

Even though life can seem too tough, or pointless, and there is a wanting to end feelings of misery, there is truth in the cliché 'there is light at the end of the tunnel'. The following poem is about someone who eventually turned their life around, found reason and purpose in life, but mainly found and followed their spiritual path.

She's gone…

It was a cold winter's night freshly fallen snow lay virgin on the ground glistening under the streetlights,

Christmas trees could be seen colourful, through the windows of houses, silence filled the air and there was a warmth coming from the family gatherings all around except in one house.

Coldness, loneliness, and sadness so deep hung so heavy, so thickly in the air.

She took a walk to escape the solitude but only felt more alone when seeing the happy filled homes.

Gazing at the water her eyes followed the ripples stretching to the other side and she felt herself being pulled along with them, her feet becoming unsteady and her balance uneasy.

She could have held on, she could have pulled herself back.

But to what? For what?
No one came, no one cared.
No one listened loneliness was all she had to live for!
And that, against the welcome of heaven's warmth...
Held no competition.

So, you see there is always hope! When everything seems lost, connecting to inner strength allows you to find that light.

Anticipation or being enthusiastic is an emotion involving pleasure, also anxiety, connected to an expected or longed-for good event. This emotion can also include irritation at being kept waiting! Excitement is also connected to Anticipation, waiting eagerly for something you know is going to happen. It can also refer to something you'd like to prevent from happening, such as the anticipation of having to do a tax self-assessment! Either way, it's a way of looking ahead to an expected or possible future.

If you have been waiting and looking forward to something for an exceptionally long time, you may have heard someone say, 'You watch when I finally get it, I will probably die' (not seriously!). The reason behind this is our subconscious awareness of an impending ending. Although we are pleased that we have finally received our awaited holiday, gift, new home etc, it is only the anticipation that has now ended! So being aware of this, we can fully appreciate our gift etc without the attachment of impending doom!

Anticipation is also identified connected to grief; this is called Anticipatory Grief. If someone you care for has or has had a terminal illness, this anticipatory grief would have begun on the day of diagnosis. Not being certain of the future, in respect of finding a cure or possible death, also wanting to have hope, although also identifying hopelessness.

The physical aspects of anticipatory grief could include crying, insomnia, and tingling. Emotional aspects could include sadness, numbness, guilt, anxiety, hopelessness, and fear. Cognitive aspects include flashbacks and coping mechanisms, such as calling it a learning experience and rationalising the experience. It is important to note that no two people are the same, however, and therefore we may all have different mourning processes or rituals (Kumar, 2005).

Dreams…

Shall I take you to a place where roses grow, with smiling faces all aglow?

Where the sun is shining and love abounds, and happy people are all around.

Where the sky is blue and the birds all sing, where the air is fresh and so lingering.

The place I speak of I've never seen, but one day soon,
And not only in dreams.

Fear is the word used to describe our emotional reaction to something that seems dangerous. Although the word fear is used in another way too, to name something a person often feels afraid of. People fear things or situations that make them feel unsafe or unsure. Or simply the unknown.

Mattered.
You mattered,
Your opinion of me mattered,
Your recognition of me and your pride in me mattered.
Your silence filled me with fear as I did not receive what I felt I needed from someone who I thought mattered.
So, that made me feel worthless, useless.
I was lost.
Someone then told me it does not matter that I don't matter, to that person as long as I mattered to me.
So, I gave myself recognition and I gave myself pride.
I then mattered...to me.
And you? You did not matter, anymore.

Loneliness is an unpleasant emotional response to perceived isolation. As a personal emotion, loneliness can be felt even when surrounded by other people; one who feels lonely is lonely. The causes are varied and can include social, mental, emotional, and environmental factors.

Loneliness is also an individual feeling about the gap between a person's desired levels of social contact and their actual level of social contact. It refers to the perceived quality of the person's relationships. Loneliness is never welcomed and reducing these feelings can take some time.

> ***I call to you…***
> *As far as the farthest shore as high as the highest summit*
> *My soul reaches out to you around every bend, every corner over and under every obstacle nothing stands in the way of my emotions.*
> *My physical entity cannot reach you. There are too many boundaries so, spiritually I call to you.*
> *Hear me, close your eyes and concentrate,*
> *it is not the whistle of the wind, or your imagination playing tricks on you!*
> *Hear my words, whispering my love for you,*
> *words of comfort and reassurance*
> *allowing me to sustain you,*
> *through your darkness and your fears,*
> *I am with you in mind, if not in body,*
> *never feel alone, never feel afraid,*
> *close your eyes, think of me, call to me,*
> *I will hear you, and you will hear me,*
> *telling you that I love you, and not to worry,*
> *and that time will end this loneliness.*

Jealousy usually refers to the thoughts or feelings of insecurity, fear, and concern over a relative lack of safety or possessions, it can consist of one or more of other emotions such as: resentment, inadequacy, or helplessness. Jealousy is separate from envy, although the two definitions have become similar, jealousy now is defined by the explanation once used for envy.

An experience of jealousy for many people may involve:
Fear of loss.

Suspicion of or anger about a perceived betrayal.

Low self-esteem and sadness over perceived loss.

Uncertainty and loneliness.

Fear of losing an important person to another.

Distrust.

An experience of envy involves:

Feelings of inferiority.

Longing.

Resentment of circumstances.

Ill will towards envied people often accompanied by guilt about these feelings.

Motivation to improve.

Desire to possess the attractive rival's qualities.

Disapproval of feelings.

Sadness towards others' accomplishments.

Jealousy is a typical experience in human relationships and has even been observed in months old infants. Scientists identify that jealousy is seen in all cultures and is universal. Although it has also been claimed that jealousy is a cultural emotion.

Sociologists have demonstrated that cultural beliefs and values play an important role in determining what triggers jealousy and what constitutes socially acceptable expressions of jealousy.

Jealousy has been explored throughout history in songs, plays, poems, books, photographs, paintings, and films, aimed at gaining a simple understanding of this complex emotion.

Let me explain…
When your mind thinks your cup is full
but it's empty
when you think there is a last step
but there is not
when your arms fold to hold something tiny
but emptiness is all that you've got.
When to look and see your own bonsai
Of eyes and smiles of a child
becomes a yearning deep in your existence,
that jealousy could make you go wild.
When days are filled with parents
with children in some sort of play,
vacating the situation is preferable.
Yet life is every which way.
You turn every cheek and all corners
to ease pain that you cannot vacate
and learn to live a life of pretence,
whilst enduring the 'Pray and wait'
Your hope is to end all farces,
of the 'Not wanting now'
and the 'I'm fine's!'
and to join the ranks of normality,
by bridging the gap
between your mind's enemy lines.
But life goes on in abundance,
and you are not in the race,
instead, you are always on the side-lines,
holding a persona up to your face.
And all the people you know,
prefer to ignore all your anguish and pain

*so, you finally realise it's simpler
to 'throw the towel in' and go around again!
Ah! But that's when you're told you need therapy,
and that a stranger can cure all your woes
and you also get given tablets,
to put a curl in your mouth and your toes!
So, for the sake of all those around you
and not forgetting sanity as well
you just keep taking the tablets,
to prevent everyone from a life of hell!*

If you have been conditioned to accept a life that others have outlined for you, your future, and your identity, it is initially difficult to see beyond this. Although your life is your life, and you are capable of much more than others' plans and expectations for you. You can rid yourself of the 'old ways' of thinking and forge a completely different future for yourself! Therefore, there is no need to be jealous of anyone when you are living your own dreams.

Disgust is an emotional response of rejection or revulsion to something considered offensive, distasteful, or unpleasant. In the book, *Expression of the Emotions in Man and Animals*, Charles Darwin identified disgust as: '*A sensation that refers to something revolting.*'

The emotion of disgust has apparently evolved as a response to foods that may cause harm to our bodies. An example of this is identified in human beings in their reaction when smelling sour milk or congealed meat. Disgust appears to be triggered by objects or people who possess attributes that signify disease (Oaten, et al. 2009).

I like what I like…
I like what I like
and I think because I want to
Shallowness bores me, and cruelty abhors.
I revel in simple things,
like bird song, and running streams.
I appreciate the sun, and tolerate the rain.
Music lifts my soul, and candles soften me.
Daylight energises me, and the darkness brings courage.
I gain my happiness from solitary places,
without competition or envy.
I am at my happiest
when I am around like-minded
and kindred spirits.

Surprise means to impress someone forcibly through unexpectedness. Also, causing an effect through being unexpected but not necessarily unusual or novel, i.e., being surprised to find someone at home early.

Do you remember?
Where you were…
If you do not
how do you know
how far you have come?
Take a moment to reflect on the past,
a glimpse of what was,
when you did not know what was to be.
Faith and courage brought you here
and will take you beyond.
You came from the depths,

and now you shine like a beacon!
You did not realise you were capable of this!
And yet here you are!
A reminder to polish occasionally
is all you need now!

Trust exists in interpersonal relationships, as humans have a natural disposition to trust and to judge trustworthiness. This can be traced to the structure and activity of the human brain. Some scientific studies have shown that trust can actually be altered e.g., by the application of oxytocin.

In a social context, trust has several connotations. Definitions of trust typically refer to situations characterised by the following aspects: One party (trustee) is willing to rely on the actions of another party (trustee), and the situation is typically directed to the future (Hardin, 2002).

A Message…
Softly she spoke
like a whisper on the wind,
words
of encouragement and promises.
Be brave little one,
for I see your tomorrows
that you cannot yet.
Immerse yourself in the music of your soul,
and allow it to diminish the thunder in your heart.
A new dawn awaits, be patient,
have faith and believe that
one day all will be well.

And now to explore the emotion of happiness, so below is a poem reflecting this.

One Day…
One day I allowed myself to feel
what it would be like
to feel happiness again
and how that would feel.
A dozen suns filled the sky,
brightness and warmth
reflected my inner self-
stretching, breathing, awakening.
A desire to run, to jump,
to scream with delight
making me realise
how suffocated I had felt spiritually,
by my darkness.
A smile engulfed my face,
relief sank into my heart,
my soul feeling quenched
after so much emotional thirst.
And then, the exhaustion afterwards,
making me feel lightheaded and weak
so much love cannot be understood by some,
because they don't know of it yet,
   but one day they will!

Happiness is always possible after everything anyone has experienced.

'Love' is not considered an emotion; in fact, some theorists define love as a choice! In that, we can choose to love someone or choose not to! Although the author defines love as simply energy, and therefore we can become aware of love's presence, so, love is a feeling, not an emotion.

Many authors, songwriters, artists and poets have described love as powerful.

The power of love: a force from above', to quote one.

Learning to love yourself means acknowledging that energy, and then accepting this love into your life and embracing it, furthermore, accepting that you are worthy of this love and so accepting yourself and all that you are.

You are far more than what you see reflected back when you look into a mirror, you have inner strength, and infinite possibilities, within you. You are far more capable than what you have been allowed to give yourself credit for. So, choose to tap into another element of yourself where all this empowerment lies.

Never Say Never...
Never say never
allow yourself to dream,
don't dwell on the past
or what might have been.
Giving up hope only allows for despair,
whatever you want is within reach out there.
Remember the passion you felt long ago,
bring it all back then allow it to grow.
A heart is a pulse that beats in time,
to all your desires whatever reason or rhyme.
Remind your soul how good it would feel,
to realise its hopes
and then make them all real

build your future on possibilities
because all that you want
can be achieved with ease.
Have faith in everything
and a happy ever after,
and before you know it
all smiles and laughter.
So do not give up,
And your heart, you can teach
that the happiness you seek,
is well within reach.

Section Four
Spirituality

A particular quote that personifies Spirituality for me is:

We are not physical beings having a spiritual experience,
We are spiritual beings having a physical experience.

– Pierre Teilhard de Chardin

The word Spirituality often makes people think of religion, (belief in something separate from themselves, being God, Jesus, or Allah to name a few religious icons). Although from a spiritualist perspective, being spiritual is having a belief in oneself.

In fact, if we compare spirituality to science, science conducts experiments in order to gain proof, although similar to religion which relies on faith and belief, spirituality also relies on faith and belief, which is possibly where the connection has derived.

Having belief in ourselves is identifying we are all-powerful beings in our own right, capable of achieving anything we set our mind to. In addition, each of us is here to discover our true selves, essentially, we are spiritual beings who have taken manifestation in physical form, although there is a path to higher consciousness (higher self) which we can discover that allows all of us to realise our infinite potential (Chopra, 2019). The higher self is the purest spiritual essence of who you are and is created from divine source energy, so to open up and connect to it means you have access to divine powers (Jones, 2008). Some choose to call this higher self, the God/Allah/Great Spirit within us.

When we are born, our awareness is focussed on ourselves, we are only aware of our survival needs, we do not focus or worry about how these needs are going to be met, we simply accept they will be. Spirituality is similar to this, in the respect that we do not have to force anything, and that we simply have to allow things to be.

Expectations and attachment play a huge part in our being and have a huge impact on our emotions. Who we think we should be, what we think we should own, and where we think we should strive to? In addition, once we have achieved these expectations that have been placed upon us, we then fear their loss, thinking that these things give us our identity and our worth. Yet even after striving for numerous years to achieve these goals, we still find ourselves not happy and not fulfilled. We place too much emphasis on what we should accumulate and own and very little on what we can give. No amount of money or possessions will ever bring everlasting happiness, this element of happiness is short-lived and so therefore one is still left feeling empty. Lasting happiness comes from giving, not receiving, it is a contentment felt deep within us, our very being, our source, our spirituality.

We exhaust ourselves trying too hard to prove to other people how beautiful we are, how clever we are, how intelligent we are, and further, how much we have achieved, how much we have accomplished, and how much money and possessions we have accumulated. Once we feel we have enough, we expect that we have succeeded, and then go on to advertise and display our success, only to be greeted with inadvertent jealousy and resentment! Why? Because it is you that has achieved this and not them! People move the goalposts all the time! So, you will never ever reach them! These expectations you possibly place on yourself were learned in childhood when possibly attacked verbally, physically, or emotionally. These limited capabilities (the knowledge and understanding of a child) caused you to react from hurt and anger, and so this became the driving force. These unhealthy emotions then became the cornerstone on which the future was built! Your being!

The 'I will show you' attitude became the internal dialogue, and so let us identify that the person who planted these weed seeds will never celebrate your success! Because their driving force is their own suppressed hurt and anger! Therefore, insulting and hurting others offers them interim relief. Whilst pursuing the exhaustive never-ending journey of acceptance, it was not noticed that the nearer one got to their goal, the goalposts were being moved further and further back!

As an adult, once the realisation of this has been acknowledged and accepted, you can then allow yourself to express any anger and pain attached. To reiterate, we do not point a finger or lay any blame, because it is no longer about them, and so focus is only on healing. Acknowledgement and acceptance can come in many forms including writing, *A no-send letter*, to whoever you deem to be the person or persons who took charge of the goalposts. This letter should include how you have been made to feel, and how that has affected your life, do not hold anything back, and in expressing these emotions you will allow a release of these historic hurts.

Sounds too simple? Although this is not so, because when you truly connect to your emotions during this exercise, you will feel again this historic pain and also the present pain connected to this realisation. So, stick with it and allow yourself to feel these emotions because this is them being released.

Write your very deepest thoughts and feelings about a particular traumatic experience in your life or an extremely emotional issue that has affected you. In your writing, really let go and explore your deepest emotions and thoughts. You might want to write about your relationships with significant others, including parents, lovers, friends, or relatives from your past or your present or even to yourself, to who you have been, who you are now and who you would like to be, or you may write about the same issues on each day of writing or even about different issues on different days. Do not worry about your spelling or grammar, the only rule is that once you begin writing, you continue until you feel you have said everything you needed to.

This letter can then be put aside when you feel overwhelmed and picked up again when you have composed yourself, or in fact, *Connected to your inner strength*. This is your spirituality, these smouldering embers deep inside of you, which with every act of courage will fan those embers until you reach your own goal of a roaring furnace! Compare this fire within you to sunshine, bringing nourishment to the roses and enriching your brain garden. You are stronger than you think you are and have more emotional strength than you have ever been allowed to believe and tapping into those embers is your gateway to emotional freedom. You have this within you but have never been made aware of it. Once you have this awareness and choose to connect to this inner strength, this then becomes the cornerstone of improving self-esteem and self-worth. You have an inner knowing of who you are, intuitively, but never before being able to identify or use this, you have possibly lived in conflict, of who you truly are and who others have told you to be. Sit in silence and connect to this source of energy to ask any questions you feel you need answering, and the answers will come! This is you connecting to you, to your higher self who has your back! And your best interests at heart.

Once you decide to trust in yourself, you will be rewarded with the answers you seek. You will begin to gain control of you! And no more will you be controlled by someone else's own inner demons and turmoil and so become master of your own thoughts and destiny. *Choices* and decisions will become your own based on your own needs and wants and you will be able to disconnect from other people's rules and regulations about how you should live your life, how you should act, think, and feel, and your driving force then becomes your own.

People thrive when they can look inside themselves and find their own solutions.

A holistic counsellor acknowledges that the human spirit is involved in the healing of the person in total: mind, body, and spirit, and although some clients possibly lean toward religion, many are now choosing to incorporate the spiritual aspect alongside their own beliefs, and rather than seeing this as a betrayal, this is being accepted as an added benefit. Marianne Clyde from the Centre for Holistic Psychotherapy reassures people of this, and as an ordained minister she feels strongly about the role that the human spirit plays in healing.

Although Carl Rogers personifies spirituality within the therapeutic relationship for the author personally when he talks of being in touch with a transcendent spiritual order.

When I am closest to my intuitive self, when I am somehow in touch with the unknown in me when perhaps I am in a slightly altered state of consciousness when I can relax and be close to the transcendental core of me, then I may behave in strange and impulsive ways in the relationship, ways that I cannot possibly justify rationally, which have nothing to do with my thought processes. But these strange behaviours turn out to be right in some odd way: it seems that my inner spirit has reached out and touched the inner spirit of the other. Our relationship transcends itself and becomes a part of something larger. (Rogers, no. 2 (1979): 98–107).

Many more therapists have also suggested that our thoughts are from a spiritual nature deriving from the soul, and Norman Doidge too gives us the information: that hidden inside each of us are energy systems, which is a gateway to healing.

Native American Shamans are ancient healers and have spoken of the mystical power of the mind and spirit. Although many have come to judge these views as too ancient, research has confirmed it appears they were on to something spiritual.

Falun Gong is another spiritual movement founded by Li Hongzhi in China around 1992.

Spirituality is not a new concept, it is something that is simply yet to be embraced as much as any other new idea or invention even, and so the more popular this becomes, the less people will be afraid to entertain this belief.

People feel at the mercy of their thoughts, and yet these thoughts have simply been put there by us or someone else, like for instance, finding a visitor's dog has left excrement in your flowerbed after they have departed. You now have a *choice*! Do you choose to leave it there, and simply complain, allowing yourself to feel disrespected or violated? Or do you choose to search out a spade and rid yourself of this unpleasant blot on your landscape?

And this is where taking back control begins, to choose a continuation of feeling uncomfortable, or to choose to take back control? THE CHOICE IS YOURS!

You enter the world with no preconceived ideas, all trusting, not suspecting, or knowing that there is a possibility you may be given or learn incorrect information so for that reason you begin your life believing that everything you learn and absorb from your parents is correct.

This is, of course, acceptable to you until it becomes time to leave the safety and sanctity of your mother's arms and venture out into the world as in starting nursery (or kindergarten). It is here that you receive different messages other than those of your parents, and so what you had accepted as factual now possibly begins to be questioned by others. It can be as simple as the parent's still allowing their child to use a dummy (or a pacifier) and yet this is taken away from the child as soon as the parent leaves, by the person in charge. The child could possibly become distressed at that moment and this could be construed as him/her resisting acceptance at having this taken away, although what this child is experiencing at that moment, is being in receipt of a visual message telling the child that 'it is not okay to have this'.

The child, at that moment, is trying to understand that changes happen, and eventually after several visits, this will cause another neural pathway to connect with the understanding of 'I am not allowed to use my dummy/pacifier here'.

This learning of 'understanding and accepting' different views other than those of your parents took time, and this continued throughout your life, each time you came across someone or something that disagreed or objected to your original learned behaviour which you absorbed from your parents.

This naturally would cause confusion and upset as it is 'going against the grain' and journeying through life you would have, and even still will, experience the same. When you are confronted with differing opinions and beliefs, they trigger frustration because this information is something you are unaware of and so do not understand, although as previously mentioned beliefs are not set in stone!

If we take time to pay attention to ourselves and listen to what we are telling ourselves, this is spirituality, your instinct, and your core being. Rather than decide if it is the beliefs you gained from your parents or is it this new information you are receiving which is correct, ask yourself! Reflect on your own consideration of this fact, explore your own pros and cons of this subject, and so reach your own conclusion and your own *choice* in this matter.

Once you have made your *choice*, then follow a decision: to change. Although we do not simply rely on our mental abilities to do this, we tap into our inner strength and focus on our own wants and needs. Our own opinions and beliefs could differ greatly from those of our parents, our work colleagues or even our current friendships and relationships.

Be aware that once we begin to connect with what makes us truly happy this possibly will not make significant people in our lives happy!

Animals give us a classic example of learned behaviour because they are trained from a very young age and very small in size. Most outdoor animals are tied with rope or chain to a post in order to keep them from wandering off and no matter how much they pull and twist to free themselves, unfortunately, they are not strong enough to break that which is keeping them attached to this post, or even uproot the post. Thus, they eventually learn that there is no point in trying anymore.

Years pass and these animals grow taller and stronger and yet this restraint (now tiny in comparison to a huge elephant or a stallion) still keeps them tethered to the spot. Purely because of this learned behaviour of 'I cannot escape'. Although of course, they can! And all it takes is disconnecting from the old beliefs and connecting to new healthier beliefs.

Although we do not disconnect first and reconnect second, we focus on connecting to new beliefs and the old beliefs simply disconnect as we do so, by lack of attention! Think of it like caring for a houseplant, if we give it attention like placing it where it will thrive whether in sunlight or shade and give it nourishment by way of water, of course, it will survive and even thrive. But, if we were to not give it water or sunshine, eventually it would wither away and die. And that is not by doing something, it is by doing nothing! Lack of attention! This is the same concept used in our brain with our neural pathways, if we do not use it, we lose it!

Once we have identified our own beliefs and passions, we can begin to introduce these to our brain, because the brain is simply a muscle, the servant, and the spirit is the master. The brain obeys instructions and whatever instructions are received rightly or wrongly it will obey and keep obeying (automatic pilot) until you change the information. Like any other muscle in our body, we have the control to change its structure, and anything that has been done to the brain can be undone.

So let us change it! Begin by constructing three columns on a sheet of writing paper and in the first column list down what you want to happen/change and then not relying on your mental ability but your spiritual ability, write down beside each item on the list (in the second column) a mantra that you can identify, to consolidate this new belief. Remember a mantra is simply the practice of repeating the same words over and over (and repetition is the mother of all learning!).

Once you have identified your new hopes and dreams, write down your corresponding mistaken beliefs in the third column. If you wish you could put a heading for each i.e., Column one – New Habit, Column two – Changes That Will Happen, and in column three – Old Habit. Because that is all this old way of thinking is – a habit that needs changing!

Each time you have a negative thought connected to your old habit, your mantra over and over and over until your attention is taken over by something else happening in your life. In fact, you do not even have to wait for a negative thought to appear. You can recite your mantra whilst doing anything else monotonous or at bedtime even and the monotone will even help you fall to sleep! You could choose to write your mantra on 'post-it notes' and place them on your bathroom mirror, wardrobe door, or car dashboard, you could even decide to put a mantra as a screensaver on your laptop or phone because it is not just the verbal that send messages or signals to our brain it is the visual too, and each similar message resonates with an already connected positive neural pathway causing it to lengthen and thicken and eventually this new message will become the automatic pilot.

You CAN bring about these new changes in your life! All it takes is commitment, dedication and repetition!

All this effort goes towards fanning those smouldering embers of your inner strength, making it the roaring furnace that you deserve it to be. The heat from your furnace acts as the sunshine for you to nourish and grow your positive thought roses.

We could liken the aspects of our being i.e., Physical, Mental, Emotional, and Spiritual to all the four elements, earth, wind, fire, and water. We could associate the physical aspect to earth, the solid foundation of being, the mental we could connect to water, in the respect of our thoughts which can be manageable like a calm stream at times and at other times we can feel flooded and overwhelmed by the volume, at other times our thoughts can feel unmanageable like water escaping from a burst dam. NATs are the fluid nourishment that keeps the negative neural pathways alive and thriving. Emotions we could identify as wind, when a hurricane of various emotions presents, leaving us feeling shaken up and exhausted. And lastly the spiritual, of course, we can connect to fire, our inner strength.

Our awareness of self begins with the physical; our physical nourishment needs for survival (to be kept fed and warm), and our awareness then extends to our mental needs, of what we need to know personally in order to keep on surviving. Emotional needs are not given as much attention by self or others as long as our physical needs are being met and our spiritual needs are generally ignored.

As we need to nourish all aspects of our being in order to feel content, equal attention has to be paid to all. Similarly, to a car with four wheels, it can run on a flat tire or even two, although the journey will be a struggle, just like living life possibly feels. Life can feel difficult and frustrating because we are not paying attention to all four aspects of being (tires).

Mindfulness is sometimes referred to as spiritual mindfulness because you are paying attention to your spiritual self, you are connecting and listening to you! And your own needs, wants, desires, and passions. It is about paying attention to you!

We can feel burdened by the weight of so many other people's rules and opinions of how we should live our lives, how we should think, and how we should feel, and yet aside from this your opinions are absent. So, it is time to offload, removing all that you have absorbed from others that no longer serve you. People will judge and offer advice in absence of personal boundaries, although conformity is not authentic! We can listen but then we need to gain faith in self in order to pursue our authentic self. Cease to rely on anyone else; empowerment comes from responsibility, relying on yourself to do what is best for you. Life will begin to make more sense to you when you start to listen to you!! And discover the core truth of who you really are (Ramsay, 2018).

As you become better at doing this you will begin to feel better, connect to your inner strength, which is your higher self, one that is not controlled from the external, the you that you can rely on for guidance, strength, knowledge, faith, belief, understanding, trust in yourself and know that you have your best interest at heart to reach your own goals. You are your own best friend, you are your number one, not your partner, or your children, or your parents, you have to prioritise yourself before anyone and everyone else in your life, and everyone else comes after in whatever order you choose.

When we begin to prioritise, this does not mean we stop caring about others, it simply means we begin to care about ourselves first and foremost, and it is okay to do that, you are allowed to give yourself permission to do so; this is not bad, this is a necessity, to promote self-care. And when you become your ultimate best, you will have more energy to devote to your loved ones, whilst always having the awareness to also love yourself.

You can either choose to re-prioritise, or you can also choose to completely disconnect from people in your life who you feel exerts too much control over you. Unfortunately, people are too bogged down with constructs that they feel they are not allowed to prioritise themselves at all, thinking that they have to accept this disrespectful behaviour from parents or others, simply in the name of 'duty'. Although you have a duty to yourself first and foremost! And when we begin to promote self-care and create personal boundaries our priorities change. It is about letting yourself know that you are allowed to do this and giving yourself permission to look after yourself first.

For too long, you have been ignoring your wants and your needs, and now is the time to start paying attention, and start listening to you!

You are allowed to be selfish!

Focuses on you, become aware of you, ask yourself:

'What do I want?'

'What do I need?'

Although in doing this, you have to take time out, sit in silence, and connect to you!

You have possibly heard the expression, *Finding yourself,* well that is exactly what you need to do! Below all the constructs, below everyone else's opinions and beliefs, lies your own, lies you! For a moment, forget thinking about your job, your partner, your commitments, your parents, and think about you! Make time for yourself and if you need to lock yourself in a room to do this, then do it, if you need to go and sit in a park or on a hilltop to give yourself space from responsibilities and commitments, and then do so.

When you begin to pay attention to yourself and listen to your own thoughts about you, you will discover what it is that is holding you back from having a better quality of life, this is where you decide on what changes you are going to implement in your life, to take better care of you.

You may discover during this reflection that it is not simply things in the present that are preventing you from moving toward a brighter future, maybe choosing to change jobs, moving home, or deciding to end an unhealthy relationship, you could possibly discover that it is the old thought process and habits that are preventing you from believing you are allowed to. A feeling of being stuck, grounded in the past, and the thought of bringing about changes are met with resistance and fear.

Of course, how do you know if these changes you are going to implement are going to work out for the best? You do not! But does that mean you cannot decide to change it again?

Confusion, frustration, and indecisiveness can lead to feelings of anxiety, although in focusing on only yourself you can bring clarity to the situation, making it all about you, reorganising your thoughts so they all meet up at the same point: How does this benefit ME!? If it does not, let it go.

Choose your favourite colour and make your thought preferences that colour, pleasant and solid, then assign all other thoughts different colours depending on where or who these thoughts have originated from. Next, you could group together the corresponding colours (This can either be done as a visual thought process or at a convenient time using paper and coloured pens, or both). What you are doing here is assigning importance, and discovering those thoughts that require your least attention, possibly identified by your least favourite colour?

Once you have separated your blockages into neat little coloured piles (like you would with a week's mass of dirty laundry) it will be easier to deal with them individually and so then you can choose to prioritise or disregard.

We would not attempt to bundle an entire week's laundry into the washing machine all in one go, yet we expect ourselves to deal with a similar multitude of thoughts in one go!

Talking of colours, this links us to another aspect or belief of our spiritual being, in the form of chakras.

Yogi Cameron, a yoga and Ayurvedic therapist, give us an insight into these seven chakras (which are considered the main energy centres of the body that promote harmony between our physical, mental, emotional, and spiritual aspects).

Each chakra has a corresponding colour, meaning and purpose. Blocked energy in any of these seven chakras is thought to be a cause of the feeling of being 'stuck'.

Oh, Ayurvedic medicine is one of the world's oldest holistic healing systems and was developed more than 3,000 years ago in India. It is based on the belief that health and wellness depend on a balance between the mind, body, and spirit.

So, these seven chakras (or energy centres) are generally identified as the following:

- *Root Chakra* (Muladhara) RED.
- *Sacral Chakra* (Swadhisthana) ORANGE.
- *Solar Plexus Chakra* (Manipura) YELLOW.
- *Heart Chakra* (Anahata) GREEN.
- *Throat Chakra* (Vishuddha) BLUE.
- *Third-eye Chakra* (Ajna) INDIGO.
- *Crown Chakra* (Samsara) VIOLET.

The root chakra represents 'foundation'. It anchors us and gives us the feeling of being grounded. When the root chakra is open, we feel confident in our ability to withstand challenges and stand on our own two feet.

This chakra is located in the base of the spine, in our tailbone area.

Sacral Chakra:

The sacral chakra helps inform how we relate to our emotions and the emotions of others. An open sacral chakra also governs creativity and sexual energy and is located in the lower abdomen.

Solar Plexus Chakra:

The solar plexus chakra speaks to your ability to be confident and in control of your life; the location of this chakra is in the upper abdomen in the stomach area.

Heart Chakra: The heart chakra is one of the most important chakras since it connects the bottom three chakras (associated with materiality) with the top three ones (associated with spirituality) This chakra can influence our ability to give and receive love, although it is situated in the centre of the chest and just above the heart.

Throat Chakra:

The throat chakra gives voice to the heart chakra and controls our ability to communicate, and allows us to express ourselves clearly. Of course, this is located in the throat.

Third-Eye Chakra: The third-eye chakra speaks to our ability to see the big picture and connect to intuition. Think of it as the eye of the soul and is located on the forehead centre to our eyes.

Crown Chakra:

The crown chakra, the highest chakra, represents our ability to be fully connected spiritually. When you fully open your crown chakra, it is thought that we can gain access to a higher consciousness. This Chakra is situated above your head.

And now for a little background information on where this belief originated.

The Sanskrit word, *Chakra,* translates to, *Wheel*, or *Circle*. It may also refer to a whirlpool or whirlwind (chakravakam). In the West, we are most familiar with the Muladhara, or seven-chakra system, but there are any number of systems and maps with their own colours, symbols.

The chakras and Kundalini came to be an integral part of yoga philosophy in the non-dual Tantric tradition, which arose in the seventh century, in reaction to the dualist philosophy which preceded it. This tradition advised being in the world rather than being separate from it. Tantra is commonly thought of in the west as primarily a sexual tradition, as Tantrism does put sexuality in a sacred context. Yet, this is actually only a small part of a broad philosophy, which includes many practices of yoga, worship of deities, especially the Hindu goddesses, and integration of the many Polaric forces in the universe.

The main information about chakras that have come to us in the west is a translation by the Englishman, Arthur Avalon, in his book, *The Serpent Power*, published in 1919. These texts: the Sat-Chakra-Nirupana, written by an Indian pandit in 1577, and the Padaka-Pancaka, written in the tenth century, contain descriptions of the centres and related practices. There is also another tenth-century text, called the Goraksha Satakam, which gives instructions for meditating on the chakras. These texts form the basis of our understanding of chakra theory and Kundalini yoga today (Judith, 2019).

The description 'Energy Centres' is derived from Traditional Chinese Medicine (TCM), although the development of TCM follows a different process from that of modern science, so it is more likely impossible to completely define the intricacy of TCM using the perspectives and research methods of modern western science! Also, energy cannot be directly observed, it has no clear boundaries!

The human body includes both visible and invisible parts. The former is the material system, and the latter is the energetic system (in addition to consciousness, as mentioned briefly above). As matter and energy can be converted into each other, it is important to study the human body from the perspective of both the material and energetic systems, which can complement each other. The nature of the energetic system is different from that of the material system.

The TCM perspective is based on energy; therefore, extending research on the human energy system may lead to the establishment of a modern TCM research field that is firmly grounded in the principles of TCM. Such a research field might generate novel findings (Liu, 2018).

The east of the globe including China, Tibet, Thailand, and Japan embrace this information although in the west it is generally considered ancient wisdom, although this was not simply connected to a spiritual belief it is also identified with how we move, digest food, think and even feel.

Those countries that do celebrate this discovery further identify that these main energy centres are connected via a network known as energy channels, also that the flowing energy comprises of two different forces namely Yin and Yang. Along these channels are where numerous smaller energy points (known as meridians) are located, which can also become blocked by various means. This is an expansive network and runs through our entire body, and although the west is yet to embrace this theory, with the help of two specific pieces of medical equipment, specialists aim one day to measure and identify these meridians.

Locations of primary meridians have been identified as:

Lung, Large Intestine, Stomach, Spleen, Heart, Small Intestine, Urinary Bladder, Kidney, Gallbladder, Liver, Pericardium (a sack which contains fluid and surrounds the heart) and also the San Jiao meridian which is not tied to any specific organ.

A Magnetic Resonance Imaging (MRI) machine which is a type of scan that uses strong magnetic fields and radio waves to produce detailed images of the inside of the body, this MRI scanner is a large tube that contains powerful magnets, which a person lays inside during the scan. This scanner can be used to examine almost any part of the body, and the results of an MRI scan can be used to help diagnose conditions.

Also, an electrocardiogram (ECG) is a simple test that can be used to check your heart's rhythm and electrical activity. Sensors attached to the skin are used to detect the electrical signals produced by your heart each time it beats; the signals are then recorded by a machine.

So, different parts of the world are not singing from a different hymnbook, just a different page! Scientists lead the way in what is acceptable to believe or not depending on experiments to prove or disprove theories being conducted, and although faith or belief cannot be proved or disproved, researchers at Korea's Seoul National University (SNU) published an article stating that they have confirmed the existence of meridians in 2016.

While the existence of meridians and acupuncture points has not been scientifically proven by western scientists yet, research into the potential medical benefits of acupuncture, acupressure, and related treatments (TFT and EFT) has been ongoing, with new evidence emerging regularly.

Scientists at SNU also say they have confirmed the existence of what is referred to as, the *Primo-Vascular System*, which they state forms a vital part of the cardiovascular system. These researchers believe the primo-vascular system to be the physical component of the meridian system, and it has been suggested that this system is involved in channelling the flow of energy and information relayed by 'Bio-photons' and DNA.

So, onward, and upwards towards embracing any and all information that benefits us.

I cannot help though, comparing this information to that of the vagus nerve, as I find some concepts are extremely similar.

Many people choose to use crystals (or gemstones) when attempting to unblock energy centres (or chakras), the crystals are placed on the seven main energy centres (or also at each meridian point) as they meditate.

You could choose to make this crystal energy centre re-balancing a regular part of your spiritual well-being.

A crystal is a special kind of solid material where the molecules fit together in a repeating pattern; this pattern causes the material to form all sorts of unique shapes. The process of crystal-forming is called crystallisation, crystals often form in nature when liquids cool and start to harden. Certain molecules in the liquid gather together as they attempt to become stable, they do this in a uniform and repeating pattern that forms the crystal.

We can also learn from science that crystals can form when liquid rock, called magma, cools. If it cools slowly, then crystals may form. Many valuable crystals such as diamonds, rubies, and emeralds also form this way.

Quartz crystals have a natural property called, *Piezoelectricity,* an ability to generate an electrical field, which makes them especially useful in radio and video equipment. Silicon crystals are used in making the chips that power our computers and the photovoltaic cells used in solar technology.

The key differences between crystals and gemstones are that gemstones are considered rare pieces of minerals that are found underground, which are then cut and polished to be used in jewellery and other decorative pieces. Crystals are pure substances whose atoms, molecules, or ions are arranged in an ordered pattern, where they extend in all three spatial dimensions. A gem can be a crystal, while a crystal cannot be called a gem.

Gemstone and Crystals are both used in various applications in today's world. While gemstones are primarily used in jewellery and decoration pieces, crystals can be used in various applications such as healing, jewellery, vases, scientific purposes, etc.

The idea of working with crystals is based on the understanding and acceptance that each stone has the purpose of magnifying or balancing the energy centre you are focusing on. Therefore, when choosing a healing crystal, you have to consider several attributes, including energetic quality, colour, and also the intuitive or personal connection you receive from it.

The energies of particular crystals are designed to match with each of your seven energy centres, helping to remove energy blocks and create balance, crystals to consider for this purpose are:

- *Root energy centre: Bloodstone, Tiger's Eye, Hematite, Fire Agate, And Black Tourmaline.*
- *Sacral energy centre: Citrine, Carnelian, Moonstone, Coral.*
- *Solar Plexus energy centre: Malachite, Calcite, Citrine, Topaz.*
- *Heart energy centre: Rose Quartz, Jade, Green Calcite, Green Tourmaline.*
- *Throat energy centre: Lapis Lazuli, Turquoise, Aquamarine.*
- *Third eye energy centre: Amethyst, Purple Fluorite, Black Obsidian.*
- *Crown energy centre: Selenite, Clear Quartz, Amethyst.*

This type of healing is based on the idea that we can synchronise the natural vibrations of a crystal from the earth, which has been infused with earth's natural energies, with a corresponding energy centre in the body.

When specific crystals are selected for their wavelengths, they can influence the body's energy field and so can be used to heal, energise, and revitalise.

Crystals are thought to be an inexhaustible source of energy provided they are treated with respect and can hold the energetic charge of anyone and anything they have ever come in contact with. For this reason, they need to be cleansed. The more you spend time respecting your chosen crystals and cleansing them, the stronger the energy vibration will be.

You could cleanse your crystals by placing them in a bowl of water with sea salt added or even place them outside under the light of a full moon, which is another way of cleansing them. After they have been cleansed, wrap them in cloth and store them away for the next time, as you can choose to do this each time you feel the need.

Everything in the universe is energy and vibrates to a certain frequency, including you, so begin re-energising your energy centres.

If you choose to partake in this exercise, to begin, like with any form of meditation you do not wish to be disturbed so, turn off your TV, phone etc and if you choose to, you could light candles and incense and play some ambient music, next select a cushion and a thin blanket, then sit down on the floor and place your crystals next to you, (close enough so you can reach them). You can now lie down slowly with your head on the cushion and the blanket placed just above your chest, under your arms.

Breathe in and out slowly for a few moments to allow yourself to feel calm and relaxed and once you are ready, you can either have someone else or yourself place the crystals on their corresponding energy centres one by one. The best way to start balancing energy centres is to start at the root and work your way up to the crown. If they fall off, do not worry, simply place them back where they fell from. You can choose how long you wish to participate in this exercise depending on how you feel, and this can be done as often as you wish, as you cannot over energise your energy centres.

Even sceptics will benefit from doing this, as simple deep relaxation has its advantages.

To elaborate further on the ideas of the benefits of using crystals, I shall offer an insight into specific pieces suggested for specific worries or concerns. There are many websites offering this kind of information, although the following crystal explanations are sourced from thehealingchest.com also healingcrystals.com.

Crystals to Aid Depression:

Rose Quartz: Promotes self-love.

Rose quartz vibrations reach deep within the body to dispel feelings of despair and bring out feelings of happiness. Its powers release feelings of anger, fear, and resentment, opening the body to healing light. Rose quartz also brings forth feelings of hope and restores faith in a compassionate universe, also forgiveness of self for mistakes you feel you have made.

Hematite: For the protection of body and spirit.

Hematite helps to absorb negative energy and calms the wearer/carrier in times of stress or worry. Hematite is a very protective stone and is great to carry to help you stay grounded in many situations. It is also good for helping to transform negative energies into more positive vibrations.

Citrine: Raises energy, increases self-esteem, and introduces motivation.

Citrine crystals absorb negative energies from the body and environment, and this crystal never has to be cleansed of negative energy. Citrine stones disperse negative energy naturally by transmuting it and dispelling it safely into the ground.

Lapis Lazuli: Increases confidence.

Lapis lazuli crystal benefits include feelings of peace and serenity by releasing stress. Its properties also encourage spiritual journeying and enhance spiritual power. This crystal blocks psychic attacks and reflects the psychic energy back on the attacker like a mirror.

Crystals to Aid Anxiety:

Amethyst: Calms the mind.

Amethyst's healing properties support amethyst's meaning in that they help the user keep a calm, clear mind to better receive communication and guidance. Rosary beads and prayer beads are made from amethyst to promote calm during prayer and reflection. This calm mindset opens the mind of the person wearing or holding the amethyst beads to connect easier with higher forces.

Labradorite: Clears the mind of irrational thoughts.

The protective powers of labradorite stone protect the aura by creating an energy barrier, this barrier then holds personal energy in and provides protection from people who would drain or tap into that personal energy. Because of this protective barrier, elemental forces are enhanced but kept in balance. Labradorite also enhances perseverance and strength, assists in spiritual healing, and provides strength in the face of adversity.

Smokey Quartz: Promotes focus and clarity.

This crystal is excellent for relaxation and is also very grounding and protective in the working environment. It is beneficial after a period of illness because it aids in the recuperation of personal energies. It is also said to aid insomnia and bring peaceful dreams.

Blue Lace Agate: Restores inner calm, promotes relaxation.

Blue Lace Agate cleanses and stabilises the aura, eliminating negativity. Agate enhances mental function and improves concentration; it also soothes and calms inner anger and facilitates a sense of security and safety. Blue Lace Agate will boost your ability to communicate, especially the thoughts and feelings that you receive from your higher self.

It is a soothing and nurturing stone that will bring peace of mind, and it is also an excellent emotional healing stone.

And now suggestions for a crystal 'First Aid Kit':

Clear Quartz.

Green Aventurine.

Black Tourmaline.

Citrine: Description above.

Rose Quartz: Description above.

Clear quartz is highly prized for its ability to clear the mind of negativity and to enhance higher spiritual receptiveness. It is considered the master of all healing crystals due to its ability to amplify healing vibrations of other crystals; its own healing properties are also extremely beneficial in spiritual healing. This stone enhances personal awareness and growth, and its properties work subliminally to give benefits to anyone who has not yet experienced spiritual awakening although in general, it empowers everyday thoughts and feelings.

Green Aventurine comforts, harmonises, protects the heart, and can help attract love later in life. It is good for attracting luck, abundance, and success. This crystal has particularly soothing energy behind it and is recommended for working through unresolved emotional issues; it is known as a stone of personal growth and offers opportunities for learning about oneself and one's place in the universe.

The Black Tourmaline crystal transfers negative energies into positive and shields the wearer by increasing its own electromagnetic field, so any negativity is repelled. It is a good crystal to hold if you feel spaced-out, forgetful, or disoriented because it quickly centres and grounds the wearer in the present moment.

I hope this information has gone some way toward the reader embracing the benefit of crystals, and to be able to benefit fully from the positive energy of the crystals, you can either choose to wear one specific crystal or multiple (as a pendant or bracelet) or instead, choose to carry one/multiple in a purse or wallet.

Another spiritual theory to attain deep relaxation and unblock energy centres is by means of, *Reiki* (ray-key), this is a Japanese word for, *universal life energy*, and is also a word used to describe a system of natural healing, (energy centres are also referred to as chakras by Reiki Masters).

This theory was founded by Mikao Usui in the early twentieth century and is a form of spiritual practice used as an alternative therapy for the treatment of physical, emotional, and mental diseases. Mikao Usui was the creator of Reiki and taught his beliefs to over 2000 people during his lifetime; his presence continues to live by the knowledge he shared, which is still embraced by Reiki masters and practitioners in the present today.

A typical Reiki session would consist of the person sitting in a comfortable chair or lying on a therapy table with their head on a cushion and covered with a thin blanket. To create ambience lighted candles and incense could be present, also soft music may be playing in the background.

The practitioner then places their hands lightly on or over specific areas of the head, limbs, and torso for roughly five minutes, although the practitioner's hands can be placed over many different areas of the body, and for longer periods of time. If there is a particular physical injury, the hands may be held just above that wound.

A transfer of energy takes place whilst the practitioner holds their hands lightly on or over the person's body, and during this time the practitioner's hands may become warm. Each hand position is then held until the practitioner senses that the energy has ceased flowing, and so they will then remove their hands and place them over a different area of the body.

Techniques involved in Reiki have names such as: cantering, clearing, beaming, extracting harmful energies, infusing, also smoothing and raking the aura.

Some Reiki practitioners also choose to combine the use of crystals during this practice.

To offer an explanation on blocked chakras, and how this could possibly have an effect on our wellbeing, a good description comes from: The Chios Healing Level II manual.

Blocked chakras are chakras in which the upward flow of energy that usually ascends in the central energy channel through the entire chakra system has become restricted or stopped at one or more particular chakra centres. Blocked chakras do not just restrict this upward flow of energy, however, but restrict the entire flow of energy through that chakra.

Each chakra does not merely conduct the energy upwards through the central energy channel, to the next chakra above it, but also brings energy into itself from all around, conducts it through itself and then sends it to the entirety of the energy field (including the physical body). Blockage of a chakra affects both aspects of the energy flow, through the chakra, and so a blocked chakra has a very deleterious effect on the entire energy field of your patient. Generally, a patient will usually exhibit at least one, and often more, blocked chakras.

Blocked chakras coincide with certain psychological issues, with certain existential biases that the patient has adopted in their relationship to reality. These existential biases inhibit the wider range of self-awareness and action available to the patient, restricting it to a limited range of expression: the manner in which the energy in the chakra system (and the body) is similarly restricted, and cannot operate freely and effectively at certain levels, reflects the corresponding way in which the entire life process has become restricted…Unblocking chakras, in concert with other techniques, often provides a great deal of emotional healing and spiritual healing for the patient, and prevents physical disease, too (Barrett, 2011).

You may identify that one or more of your chakras are blocked, and this could be because when one is blocked, the other chakras attempt to compensate (Patel, 2019) allows us to explore this possibility and advises us of some warning signs to look out for, showing that your chakras may be out of Balance, beginning with the root chakra.

Physical imbalances in the root chakra include problems in the legs, feet, tailbone, immune system, and prostate gland. Those with imbalances here are also likely to experience issues of arthritis, knee pain, sciatica, and constipation.

Emotional imbalances include feelings affecting our basic survival needs: money, shelter, and food; ability to provide for life's necessities.

When this chakra is clear of blockages, you feel supported, a sense of connection and safety with the physical world.

The lesson of this chakra is self-preservation.

Sacral Chakra

Physical imbalances include sexual and reproductive issues, urinary problems, and kidney dysfunctions, hip, pelvic and low back pain.

Emotional imbalances include lack of commitment to relationships, inability to express emotions, express creativity or enjoy pleasurable activities, also fears of betrayal.

When this chakra is balanced, we have an ability to take risks; we are creative, and we are committed, passionate, sexual, and outgoing.

The lesson of this chakra is to honour others.

Solar Plexus:

Physical imbalances include digestive problems, liver dysfunction, chronic fatigue, high blood pressure, diabetes, stomach ulcers, pancreas and gallbladder issues, also colon diseases.

Emotional imbalances include issues of personal power and self-esteem, our inner critic comes out causing fears of rejection and self-criticism of our physical appearances.

When this chakra is balanced, we feel self-respect, in control, assertive, confident.

The lesson of this chakra is self-acceptance.

Heart Chakra

Physical imbalances include asthma, heart disease, lung disease, issues with breasts, lymphatic systems, upper back and shoulder problems, arm, and wrist pain.

Emotional imbalances include issues of the heart, fear of abandonment, fear of loneliness, anger, and bitterness.

When this chakra is balanced, we feel joy, gratitude, love, compassion, and forgiveness.

The lesson of this chakra is I Love.

Throat Chakra

Physical imbalances include problems with the thyroid, sore throats, laryngitis, ear infections and any facial problems (chin, cheek, lips, tongue) also neck and shoulder pain.

Emotional imbalances include issues of self-expression through communication, fear of having no power or choice, also having no willpower, also feelings of being out of control.

When this chakra is balanced, our words flow freely, communication is easy.

The lesson of this chakra is to speak up and let your voice be heard.

Third Eye Chakra

Physical imbalances include headaches, blurred vision, sinus issues, eyestrain, seizures, and hearing loss.

Emotional imbalances include issues with self-reflection and an inability to look at one's own fears or to learn from others.

When this chakra is balanced, we feel focused and can determine between truth and illusion. We are also open to receiving wisdom and insight.

The lesson of this chakra is to look outside the box!

Crown Chakra

Physical imbalance includes depression, inability to learn, sensitivity to light, sound, and the environment.

Emotional imbalances include issues with self-knowledge; also, imbalances arise from having a closed mind or tunnel vision.

When this chakra is balanced, we live in the present moment and have trust in our inner guidance.

The lesson of this chakra is to live reflective and mindful.

The third eye energy point has been associated with the pineal gland, which is the size of a marrowfat pea, shaped like a pinecone (which is how it got its name) and situated in the middle of the brain between the two hemispheres. It is the only energy point that is associated with a physical aspect of our body.

In spirituality, the third eye often symbolises a state of enlightenment, also the ability to see visions during meditation of spiritual or psychological significance. Also, in India, Dharmic spiritual traditions refer to 'the Third Eye' as the gate that leads to higher consciousness.

Dissection of this gland through recent medical research has identified that the front section of the pineal gland has a similar structure as our other two eyes, and so, since this discovery this gland has been referred to as: A Vestigial Eye!

Vestigial, meaning: a very small remnant of something that was once greater or more noticeable (of an organ or part of the body: degenerate or having become functionless in the course of evolution).

So, there is a recent acceptance that there is something of visual consequence connected to the pineal gland!

Although as early as the sixteenth century, we had René Descartes, who was a French philosopher, mathematician, and scientist, believing that the mind exerted control over the brain via the pineal gland! (The idea he put forward concerning a relation between mind and body is known as, *Cartesian dualism or substance dualism*). He also believed that 'mind' was clearly separate from 'matter' (physical) but could definitely influence matter!

His idea of vision and its interaction with the pineal gland concerned light rays impressing subtle particles into the eyes, and then this image was transmitted to the pineal gland, which he considered served as the connection between mind and body.

Again in 1918, Nils Holmgrenin (a Swedish anatomist) referred to the pineal gland as the 'Third Eye' because he discovered cells that looked like retina cone cells found in the tip of the gland in some frogs and dogfish sharks. And another recent discovery found that the pineal gland in the Western Fence Lizard contains a photo-receptive element scientists also chose to call, a *third eye*! (Richards, 2019).

So, the idea that the third eye energy point is directly associated with the pineal gland (which has visionary abilities) is definitely not a new-age idea! And not as far-fetched as people would like to think.

If someone decided they would like to attempt to see visions during meditation (of spiritual or psychological significance) or connect to a higher consciousness, then we are told by Gaia (2019) that this can be achieved by following four simple steps.

1. Sit quietly.
2. Let your thoughts go.
3. Speak to the higher self.
4. Be receptive.

The Higher Self is an even higher level than the soul; it is in every person ever born, and is the essence, the universe that dwells within us all, it is a source of light and life within, and our true motivation for living. The higher self is what powers us, our inner strength. The physical realm and body in which we dwell are thought to be a vessel for the higher self.

It is not a huge struggle through your willpower to contact your higher self and all you need to do is set your intention to make contact with your higher self, to open up to the possibility and receive energy, love, and inspiration. Silence is a must in this process, as this connection goes beyond the mind, and you should rid yourself of as many distractions as possible.

You may not feel you have made contact, but do not feel discouraged as it always responds to your call. Let go of any thoughts about the outer world and go within and ask your higher self to come closer. Ask for guidance or answers to worries as you enter into silence. You can do this out loud if you choose to and it is in these moments of silence that you receive much wisdom, power, and love.

Afterwards, notice what new thoughts you have after these moments of silence. You may feel like you are giving yourself a massage, although you may feel a sense of new energy, peace, inner knowing, or an answer you were seeking. Do not worry if you do not feel or identify any response, just be open to the possibility that contact has been made, simply through your intention.

It is even okay to have quick meditation periods throughout the day, just go quiet and ask for assistance or guidance, and this is the way to deepen this spiritual connection. Also, as mentioned previously, the crystal to assist in this practice is Blue Lace Agate!

So, once you have mastered the art of raising your energy, the next step is to be vigilant that others will attempt to steal this energy from you! These people are known as energy vampires! (Or mood hoovers).

You can deal with energy vampires by firstly identifying any that you have in your life and setting personal boundaries when around these people. To do this, reflect on relationships and identify if you have ever felt emotionally exhausted after being in the company of a particular person? These people manage to drain the energy of others by constantly complaining about their own problems, they also believe the world is against them and constantly blame others for their unhappiness. They manipulate conversations by constantly talking about themselves and not wanting to listen and if you do manage to get a word in, they quickly interrupt, bringing the conversation back around to them.

These are the type of people you would choose to avoid if you have the option to, but if you do not, just to remind you, the crystal to use for protection against energy vampires is Lapis lazuli!

If you should feel that you have ever been taken advantage of by an energy vampire or anyone for that matter, do not waste time focusing on revenge, let it go and just allow 'Karma' to deal with the situation.

Karma, according to Deepak Chopra, is the third spiritual law of success. (He says there are seven altogether) Karma is both action and the consequence of that action! It is cause and effect simultaneously because every action generates a force of energy that returns to us in like kind. Deepak is an expert in the field of mind-body healing; he is a speaker and author on the subject of alternative medicine. His book, *The Seven Spiritual Laws of Success*, lists the other six spiritual laws as:

1. The Law of Pure Potentiality.
2. The Law of Giving.
3. The Law of Karma.
4. The Law of Least Effort.
5. The Law of Intention and Desire.
6. The Law of Detachment.
7. The Law of Dharma.

A good read if searching for opinions on ways to live your life better.

The mind-body connection was originally thought of as holistic, complementary, or alternative medicine, although many more Scientists, Biologists, and Psychiatrists are now embracing this idea.

Dr Joe Dispenza, D.C. is a Neuroscientist, an international lecturer, researcher, and author who has been invited to speak in more than 32 countries on five continents. His drive is connected to his belief that each of us has the potential for greatness and unlimited abilities. Dr Joe also teaches that we can rewire our brain and recondition our body to go beyond our current limitations to become supernatural!

Like Norman Doidge (Scientist, Psychiatrist and Psychoanalyst) he advocates the concept of us being able to rewire our own brains to not only create a state of total healing but to use our consciousness to command our physical reality. Dr Joe did a live stream on Gaia Sphere recently talking about going from acquiring knowledge to actually applying it, resulting in dramatic shifts in our inner and outer worlds. He shared scientific insights from his newest research to assist in understanding what is truly possible in our lives.

He encourages us to meditate deeply to deepen our process of change, which in turn will change our energy from living in the past to living in the future. He explains how we can enter deeper levels of the subconscious mind and learn how to act as our own placebo. He also explains how we can alter our limited subconscious programming and habits to a more liberated state of mind and body! He also explains how we can liberate emotional energy stored in the body, and then use it to create a new destiny.

By simply changing our attitude, we can open our hearts (and connect to our inner strength) to strengthen our immune system, and so balance our autonomic nervous system by thought alone!

Another advocate of the mind-body connection and how we can heal ourselves is Dr Bruce Lipton who is a biologist and teaches about spirituality and medicine. In his book, *The Biology of Belief*, he writes about, the *shocking truth about the pharmaceutical industry* and the science called, *Epigenetics*.

Epigenetics is the belief that you can alter your genetics by modifying your behaviour and not relying on taking medications. (There is great resistance from the pharmaceutical company against this idea of course!) Epigenetics requires a healing of the consciousness, and that is something the drug companies cannot sell!

The concept of people being able to heal themselves without drugs defies the mission of big pharmaceutical companies who are driven by profit! But according to Dr Lipton, *A minimum of one-third of all medical intervention is a placebo effect, and that is the result of positive thinking, not medication!* (A.I.S, 2019).

Epigenetics is a new type of science that is growing in popularity in the scientific world, it is the study of cellular and physiological traits or the external and environmental factors, which turn our genes on and off, and in turn, define how our cells actually read those genes. It works to see the true potential of the human mind and the cells in our body. This has the potential to change your life by making you happier and healthier, with a greater sense of spiritual well-being.

Through his experience with Epigenetics, Dr Lipton tells us how to take advantage of this new science and begin living a happy and healthy life. His books are written in a straightforward manner that is easy to understand, covering everything from how your cells work, to how you can keep things like the Honeymoon Effect, lasting your entire life, all through Epigenetics!

Dr Lipton convinces us that we are not victims of circumstance, whether that is through hereditary factors, or via our environmental circumstances. So regardless of where we were born or where we live, also regardless of who our parents are, we still have the power to change ourselves.

Originally, it was told to us that our fate is connected to our genes (genetics) and happens only through the DNA code that passes from parent to child. Therefore, we had to accept things as they are, but with the introduction of Epigenetics pointing to environmental factors having a greater impact on our health, both physically and mentally, this is far more encouraging than genetic research has previously determined.

Our response to our environment covers our cells in certain chemicals (Stress = Cortisol and Love = Dopamine and Oxytocin), so we have the potential to either surround our cells in crisis messages, or in much happier alternatives. Therefore, we can choose to live in survival or creation mode.

If we are experiencing stress and so we are producing Cortisol, which remembers, is our survival chemical (and can get actually get addicted to the production of, in the fact that it simply feels familiar) although as mentioned previously, we can break free and change from being a victim of our circumstances to mastering our destiny! (Dispenza, 2020).

Dr Lipton is an advocate of the 'Fake it till you make it' quote, also 'Dress for the job you want, not the job you have!' He also encourages the use of autohypnosis to bring about the change you want to see, i.e., listening to recordings as you are falling asleep and for them to be lengthy, so as to continue whilst you are asleep. These recordings can be directed at improving mental and/or physical health, by way of communicating with our subconscious mind.

Repetition again is emphasised, connected to these positive affirmation messages whilst sleeping, but also during your waking hours, sending new messages to our brain, until our brain 'gets it'.

So, you see, we are far more powerful than we have been led to believe! Our own thoughts, feelings, beliefs, and attitudes can positively or negatively affect how we live. In other words, our own minds can affect how healthy our bodies are!

As told us by these three highly educated and informed men, namely: Dr Norman Doidge (Scientist, Psychiatrist and Psychoanalyst) who focuses on Neuroplasticity, Dr Joe Dispenza (Neuroscientist) who focuses on Neuroscience and of course Dr Bruce Lipton (Biologist) who focuses on Epigenetics.

'*Psycho*physiology' is yet another branch of neuroscience that now seeks to understand how a person's mental state and physiological responses (the way in which body parts function) interact with one another (body and mind).

A 'Physiologist' examines and monitors human organs and systems such as respiratory, nervous and heart, to diagnose and treat any disorders and long-term illnesses. Although a '*Psycho*physiologist' is concerned with the relationship between mental and physical processes (the scientific study of the *psycho*physiological interaction between mind and body).

So, a Psychophysiologist's aim is to integrate the best of conventional medicine, with complementary or alternative treatments, so that they are able to approach healing from a position that considers the whole person! Body, mind, and spirit!

Advancement in embracing a spiritual aspect of healing!

Transcranial Magnetic Stimulation (TMS) patients have even reported feelings of increased spiritual connectedness during psychophysiological coherent states. Coherence generally refers to: a state of optimal function, although in this field they use the term psychophysiological coherence because it is characterised by increased order and harmony in both our psychological (mental and emotional) and physiological (bodily) actions.

TMS is a non-invasive form of brain stimulation in which a changing magnetic field is used to cause electric current at a specific area of the brain through electromagnetic induction. An electric stimulator is connected to a magnetic coil, which in turn is connected to the scalp. The stimulator generates a changing electric current within the coil, which induces a magnetic field; this field then causes a second inductance of inverted electric charge within the brain itself. Using heart rhythm coherence feedback, patients can learn to self-generate the coherent mode and sustain genuine positive emotional states at will! Allowing them to experience emotions, which they have described as having a spiritual experience (McCraty, 2002).

Stimulating the brain, whether by magnetic currents or meditation can induce this state of extreme relaxation and harmonic bliss, leaving the recipient feeling rested and recuperated, although it is pleasing that this experience is described as, *Spiritual*, as it goes beyond expectations and any previous encounter, and that is what spirituality is! Simply opening up to the possibility of something more.

Prior to science embracing Spirituality, of course, we had and still have spiritual teachers and if you find yourself struggling and asking questions such as: What is the meaning of life? And making statements like, what is the point? Answers to these soul-searching questions can be found if you choose to open up to the teachings of these spiritual teachers.

Deepak Chopra, who was mentioned previously, is a teacher who studied medicine in India before immigrating to the United States in 1970, where he completed residencies in internal medicine and endocrinology. His first taste of alternative medicine was when he took an interest in the Transcendental Meditation movement which was founded by Maharishi Mahesh Yogi in India in the 1950s, and has been described as a spiritual movement, this is a form of silent mantra meditation, and is said to restore inner peace.

Deepak encourages each of us to discover our true selves; that essentially, we are spiritual beings who have taken manifestation in physical form; that we are not human beings that have occasional spiritual experiences, that we are spiritual beings that have occasional human experiences. He identifies that with everyone there comes a time when we need to find the source of our spiritual guidance in the divinity of our own consciousness, and we need to look beyond religious dogma to find our spirituality within ourselves.

You hold within you the power to transform your world, Deepak takes you on an inner journey to take charge of your life, overcome your obstacles, and become the best version of yourself in his, *The Path to Empowerment*, meditation programme. He implores you to discover the profound truth that you do not have to settle or live with lost dreams and encourages you to step into your power to create a life that feels meaningful, filled with possibility and aligned with your heart's deepest desires. He knows this is possible as do I. He has also written many books on the subject of spiritual empowerment.

Another spiritual teacher is Eckhart Tolle, Eckhart is not identified with any specific religion, and says he has been influenced by a wide range of spiritual works, he is the author of, *The Power of Now* and also, *A New Earth: Awakening to Your Life's Purpose*. He has been described as the most popular spiritual author in the United States, and also as the most spiritually influential person in the world. Eckhart identifies a person's first priority as being: they need to be open to the moment, to life, and that their life exists in the present moment. He recognises that if someone cannot be in alignment with the present moment, it may be time to walk away and find a career that brings fulfilment, he also identifies that people resist the freedom to enjoy life and that they must stop this.

Unhappiness ultimately arises not from the circumstances of your life but from the conditioning of your mind. By practising, the *Power of Now*, by Eckhart Tolle you will see that the moment that judgement stops through acceptance of what it is, you are free of the mind. You have made room for love, for joy, for peace. The beginning of freedom is the realisation that you are not 'the thinker' (Tolle, 2001).

Although the onus, of course, is on oneself to bring about change, others can provide the knowledge, but it is the self that has to do the work.

Your brain garden being in need of attention and you not having the tools to do the weeding and pruning cause frustration initially, and then developing possibly into anxiety and depression. But once you have sought out and identified the tools needed, this is when the hard work begins! One hour a week with a therapist can simply be identified as receiving the tools (knowledge) required to undertake this hard work, you yourself then need to set about putting this knowledge into practice (by participating in any exercise recommended, and mantras suggested).

The hard work required initially involves taking ownership for the change you seek, with commitment, dedication, persistence, perseverance and ultimately repetition! Like the saying goes, 'If a job is worth doing, it is worth doing properly!' Time spent on yourself will result in the new you, you want to become. Like every task ever undertaken by anyone who was focussed on the best results, attention to detail is of course important, and so too is a passion and desire to obtain these results, and who better to become passionate about than yourself!

You are the most important person in your life, you are your own best friend, you are priority! And you are your own number one. You deserve the best you have to offer, and the best life has to offer! You deserve to be happy and carefree, although it is no one else's responsibility to provide you with happiness, you must take ownership and responsibility to bring forth this happiness.

Once you have stood back and observed the huge task that needs to be undertaken in order to transform this weed garden from an eyesore to a prized plot, the next step is the 'choice' not to ignore, but to prioritise then comes the 'decision' to focus on what needs to be done, and lastly bringing forth the attributes required.

A successful person becomes so by their level of dedication, which signifies the commitment of this person towards achieving their life goals. Dedication implies total devotion (connecting with their passion), so a person dedicated to achieving goals undertakes lots of perseverance. Persistence, on the other hand, signifies the firm or obstinate continuance of a goal in spite of difficulty, whereas perseverance requires steadfastness in doing something despite difficulty or delay in achieving success.

You do not owe anyone else anything, but you owe yourself everything! You deserve happiness (which of course is brought about by acquiring self-love and gaining inner peace).

You are special, you are important, and you are worthy of living this life how best suits you, and no one else! You are here for a reason, you have a purpose, and above all, you owe it to yourself to recognise and embrace all of the above.

There are many areas of therapy that embrace the spiritual aspect of our being, two of which are: Transpersonal therapy and Existential therapy.

Transpersonal therapy is a holistic practice concerned with the body, mind, and spirit. Taking a holistic approach allows for viewing life and life experiences as part of the larger process of spiritual development, facilitating the growth process through a variety of means aimed at revealing the true self and inner authenticity of the client. The aim is to address mental, physical, emotional, social, creative, and intellectual needs, with an emphasis on the role of a healthy spirit in healing.

Existential therapy focuses on free will, self-determination, and the search for meaning, often centring on you rather than on the symptom. This approach emphasises your capacity to make rational choices and to develop to your maximum potential.

The existential approach stresses that:

All people have the capacity for self-awareness.

Acute Anxiety is part of the human condition.

Existential therapy is recommended for psychological problems like substance abuse resulting from an inhibited ability to make authentic, meaningful, and self-directed choices about how to live, according to the existential approach.

Interventions often aim to increase self-awareness and self-understanding.

To elaborate on spirituality, the final piece of information in this book has been retrieved from https://www.spirituology.net/

An introduction to 'Spirituology'.

Spirituality is the knowledge of yourself as being a human spirit on the path to self-realisation and reunification with the divine universal spirit. By learning to use one's spiritual abilities and to develop them into conscience and virtues, development is made towards reunification with the universal spirit (Van-Leeuwen, 2018).

Who am I?

The subject of this article is spirituology as described in the books, *Geneeskunde,* (Spirituology) by Freek van Leeuwen (2010) also, *De Levensweg*, (The path of life, Introduction to spirituology) by Freek van Leeuwen (1991).

At first glance, spirituology seems to be something that is not of this world, but in the course of this dialogue it will become apparent that, in fact, with spirituology, we occupy ourselves with the great questions of life:

Who am I?

Where do I come from?

Where am I going?

How do I give meaning to this temporary existence?

The conscious, powerful force of life.

This makes spirituology really part of something that can be experienced; albeit that it is an inner, spiritual reality; it is the reality of yourself as being a spirit in your own inner world: the conscious, powerful force of life, which now allows the meaning of these words to penetrate itself. The meaning of this temporary, material existence is for man a mystery, which you have to resolve for yourself and it is for this reason that you ask yourself these questions of life.

The spiritual abilities.

Because you yourself are the one who asks him or herself these questions, you will, in order to answer them, begin with paying your attention to the first question, which is also the key question: who am I?

That means that we have to deal with self-knowledge, with the knowledge of the very essence of ourselves. That essential subject is the human spirit as being the conscious, powerful force of life, who possesses the four spiritual abilities: especially the ability:

To observe the things around you.

To consider them within yourself by thinking and feeling.

And then, decide what you want to do with it.

In other words, we have to engage ourselves with spirituology, for spirituology is understood to be the study of the spirit, the self-knowledge as the knowledge of yourself as being the human spirit, the knowledge of the eternal being that you are yourself, the powerful force of life.

To be able to become who you are, you must first know who you are. To this end, the following topics are discussed in the field of spirituology, entirely from the spirit's point of view:

The spirit as being the conscious force of life.

Who possesses and uses spiritual abilities?

Who can thus experience a spiritual development with them?

Which not only leads to self-realisation but also to reunification with the divine, universal spirit, your spiritual origin.

Because the relation to your fellow men towards the outside (the extraverted attitude) and towards your spiritual origin within (the introverted attitude) is also part of spirituology.

Mental development and reunification:

If you are going to apply spirituology to yourself, by transforming your abilities into conscience and virtues, then you will not only be able to develop yourself spiritually (what the meaning of your existence is) but therefore also improve your understanding with your fellow human beings and finally reunite with your spiritual origin; you will be able to reunite with your eternal source from which you, as being a human spirit, once emerged and to which you are on your way back again.

For there is one main road for man: the way back to our chosen God or source, but life often takes a different course than a man thinks for himself and there are also many sideways which in fact always just motivates man:

To make choices by using his spiritual abilities,

And thereby to grow to spiritual independence.

No belief, but the description of an experience.

Spirituology stands separate from any belief or any system of thought because it is not faith nor opinion, but a description of the human spirit and of the spiritual meaning of existence on earth; this description is based on personal spiritual observations and on a comparison of these with the spiritual experiences of others.

Every person who directs his or her attention inwards can observe the described properties of the spirit, in the form of the activity of the spiritual abilities, directly within him or herself.

From yourself as being a human spirit, you now can look again at this temporary existence and learn to see it in the light of eternity.

Spirituology is a description of the meaning of this temporary existence, entirely seen from the point of view of the spirit, the eternal life.

References
Books

Beck, A. T. (1979) *Cognitive Therapy of Depression.* USA: Guildford Press.

Berne, E. (1971) *Games People Play: The Psychology of Human Relationships.* N. Z: Castle books.

Bloom, W. (2012) *The Endorphin Effect: A breakthrough strategy for holistic health and spiritual wellbeing.* London: Hachette Digital.

Breuning, L. G. (2015) *Habits of a Happy Brain: Retrain Your Brain to Boost Your Serotonin.* USA: Simon and Schuster.

Campbell, J. (2014) *The Hero's Journey.* (3rd Ed). USA: New World Publishing.

Chopra, D. (2010) *The Seven Spiritual Laws of Success: A Practical Guide to the Fulfilment of Your Dreams.* USA: Amber-Allen Publishing.

Chopra, D. (2019) *Metahuman: Unleashing your infinite potential.* UK: Edbury publishing.

Curran, A. (2008) *The Little Book of Big Stuff About the Brain: The true story of your amazing Brain.* U.K: Crown House Publishing.

Doidge, N. (2008) *The Brain That Changes Itself.* U.K: Penguin.

Frankle, V. E. (2004) *Man's Search for Meaning.* U.K: Rider-Edbury Publishing.

Gummer, A. (2015) *Play: Fun ways to help your child develop in the first five years.* U.K: Penguin (Ebury Digital).

Goldberg, R. (2013) *Drugs Across the Spectrum.* Belmont USA: Wadsworth.

Hardin, R. (2002) *Trust and Trustworthiness.* USA: Russell Sage Foundation.

Hugdahl, K. (1995) *Psychophysiology: The Mind-body Perspective.* USA: Harvard University Press,

Jones, A. (2008) *The Soul Connection: How to access your higher powers and discover your true self.* UK: Hachette.

Kazdin, A. E. (2000) Encyclopaedia *of Psychology:* USA: APA.

Kumar, S, M. (2005) *Grieving Mindfully.* USA: New Harbinger Publications.

Peer, M. (2018) *I Am Enough: Mark Your Mirror And Change Your Life.* U.K: Marisa Peer Publications.

Peirce, P. (2009) *Frequency: The Power of Personal Vibration.* USA: Atria.

Rogers, C. (1951) *Client-Centred Therapy.* London, U.K: Constable and Robins Ltd.

Rosenberg, R. (2013) *The Human Magnet Syndrome: Why We Love People Who Hurt Us.* Ireland: Premier Publishing & Media.

Tappe, N. A. (2009) *Understanding Your Life Through Colour: Metaphysical Concepts in Colours and Auras.* USA: Starling Publishers.

Tolle, E. (2001) *The Power of Now: A Guide to Spiritual Enlightenment.* U.K: Hodder & Stoughton General Division.

Journals:
Baikie, K. and Wilhelm, K. (2005) Retrieved from: "Emotional and physical health benefits of expressive writing". *Advances in Psychiatric Treatment. 11 (5): 338–346.* doi:10.1192/apt.11.5.338.

Clements-Cortes, A. Bartel, L. Ahonen, H. Freedman, M. Evans, M. Tang-Wai, D. (2017) *Can Rhythmic Sensory*

Stimulation Decrease Cognitive Decline in Alzheimer's Disease? A Clinical Study. Retrieved From: Music and Medicine Vol 9, No3 (2017)
http://dx.doi.org/10.47513/mmd.v9i3.565

Clyde, M. (2017) *Holistic Counselling on the Rise.* Retrieved from: http://careersinpsychology.org/holistic-counseling/

Dispenza, J. (2020) *Rewired: Living in Survival V Living in Creation.* Retrieved from: YouTube:
https://youtu.be/MtimAuhyP-M

Liu, T. (2018) *Journal of Traditional Chinese Medical Sciences.* Volume 5, Issue 1, January 2018, Pages 29–34 Retrieved from:
https://www.sciencedirect.com/science/article/pii/S2095754818300358

Oaten, M. Stevenson, R. Case, T. (2009). Retrieved from: *Disgust as a Disease-Avoidance Mechanism.* Psychological Bulletin. 135 (2): 303–321.

Pepperell, R. (2018) *Consciousness as a Physical Process Caused by the Organisation of Energy in the Brain.* Retrieved from: *Front. Psychol.* 9:2091. DOI: 10.3389/fpsyg.2018.02091.

Rogers, C. (1957) Retrieved from: *The Necessary and Sufficient Conditions of Therapeutic Personality Change. Journal of Consulting Psychology,* Vol. 21.

Rogers, C. (1979) *The Foundations of the Person-centred Approach.* Retrieved from: *Education* 100, no. 2 (1979): 98–107.

Terr, L. C. (1991) *Childhood traumas: An outline and overview. The American Journal of Psychiatry,* 148(1), 10–20. https://doi.org/10.1176/ajp.148.1.10

Videos:
Webpages:
A.I.S. (2019) *American Institute of Stress.* Retrieved from: https://www.stress.org/dr-bruce-lipton-shocked-the-world-with-his-discovery

Barrett, S. H. (1994–2011) *Chios Healing Level II manual.* Retrieved from: http://www.chioshealing.com/HealingLevel2/EnergyDefects/energydefects.htm

Cameron, Y. (2019) A Beginner's Guide To The 7 Chakras. Retrieved from: https://www.mindbodygreen.com/0-91/The-7-Chakras-for-Beginners.html

Deboni, M. (2021). Retrieved from: https://www.whitsundayprofessionalcounselling.com/assertive-anger-management

Ducksters. (2021) *Earth Science for Kids: Soil.* Retrieved from:

https://www.ducksters.com/science/earth_science/soil_science.php

Ekman, P. (2021) Retrieved from: https://www.paulekman.com/universal-emotions/what-is-sadness/

Gaia (2014) Retrieved from: https://www.gaia.com/article/how-connect-your-divine-energy-self-4-steps.

GoodTherapy.org (2020) Retrieved from: https://www.goodtherapy.org/blog/10-ways-to-boost-dopamine-and-serotonin-naturally-1212177

Gundersen. (2021) Retrieved from https://www.gundersenhealth.org/health-wellness/live-happy/healthy-ways-to-deal-with-sadness/

Hamilton, D. R. (2019) *Real vs. Imaginary in the Brain and Body.* Retrieved from: https://drdavidhamilton.com/real-vs-imaginary-in-the-brain-and-body/

Judith, A. (2019) *History of the chakra system.* Retrieved from:
http://cryskernan.tripod.com/chakra percent20history.htmf

Lipton, B. (2017) Retrieved from: https://www.brucelipton.com/newsletter/think-beyond-your-genes-december-2017

Lipton, B. (2019) Retrieved from:
https://www.brucelipton.com/what-epigenetics

Martel, J. (2021) Retrieved from:
https://www.healthline.com/health/passive-aggressive-personality-disorder

McCraty, C.R. (2002) Retrieved from
https://www.heartmath.org/research/research-library/basic/psychophysiological-correlates-of-spiritual-experience/

Miller, S. (2019) Retrieved from:
https://www.udemy.com/crystal-healing-practitioners-course-with-certificate/learn/lecture/9773100?start=285#

Patel, R. (2019) Retrieved from:
https://www.mindbodygreen.com/0-13433/warning-signs-your-chakras-are-out-of-balance.html

Ramsay, K. (2018) *Mindfulness.* Archaeology Ltd, Udemy, Inc.

Richards, R. (2019) *The Pineal Gland.* Retrieved from:
http://www.rickrichards.com/chakras/Chakras1d.html

Robins, C. (2019) What Is a Crystal and How Does It Form? Retrieved from: https://sciencing.com/what-crystal-how-does-form-4925052.html

Roupe, L. B. (2020) *Seven Things That Affect Your Vibrational Frequency.* Retrieved from: https://www.theatreartlife.com/lifestyle/7-things-vibrational-frequency/

Seymour, T. (2017) Retrieved from: *Everything you need to know about the vagus nerve.* Retrieved from: https://www.medicalnewstoday.com/articles/318128.php

The Healing Chest (2020) Retrieved from: https://thehealingchest.com/crystals-stones/clear-quartz-meaning/

Healing Crystals (2020) Retrieved from: https://www.healingcrystals.com/Green_Aventurine_Articles_103.html

Thalmann, P. (2004) Retrieved from: https://www.diversalertnetwork.org/medical/articles/Decompression_Illness_What_Is_It_and_What_Is_The_Treatment

Traube, M. (2017) Retrieved from: https://www.psychologytoday.com/gb/blog/healthy-mind-healthy-skin/201701/anxiety-and-your-skin

Van-Leeuwen, F. (2018) *Introduction to spirituology.* Retrieved from: https://www.spirituology.net/

Van-Rheenan, A. (2018) Retrieved from: https://www.vanrheenencounseling.com/blog-christian-counseling/5-anger-responses.